Praise for *The Lenovo Way*

"Lenovo is a truly global success by taking the best of East and West and creating an innovative global organization. In this book, the authors pull back the covers and give incredible insights into this fascinating organization of the future, sharing a blueprint that others can adapt to be a truly global organization."

—Dave Ulrich, Ross School of Business, University of Michigan; author of *HR Transformation* and *The Why of Work*

"For years, 'soft' values like diversity were undervalued in the business world, which was more focused on bottom-line hard profits than on human resources. Through groundbreaking and innovative leadership, Lenovo has proven that soft values can lead to huge profits. *The Lenovo Way* shows how they did it— and how you can too."

—Marshall Goldsmith, author of the *New York Times* bestseller *What Got You Here Won't Get You There*

"If you want to grow your business and turn global opportunity into reality, read *The Lenovo Way*. The dynamic East-West duo of Gina Qiao and Yolanda Conyers (both working mothers) has harnessed the power of diverse talent to create a corporate culture that embraces change and innovation. *The Lenovo Way* shares important business lessons for a global world."

—Carol Evans, President, Working Mother Media

"The Lenovo Way is a must read for leaders who are seeking to apply global leadership attributes in a dynamic global marketplace. It is a great display of how courageous leaders are able to apply business acumen, emotional intelligence, and cultural agility in transforming an already successful business model. Read it!"

—Ronald C. Parker, President and CEO,
Executive Leadership Council & Foundation;
former SVP of HR and Chief Global Diversity Officer, PepsiCo

"As president & CEO of an organization that is currently expanding globally, I am learning firsthand—and watching my colleagues learn—many of the important leadership and management lessons included in this book. In *The Lenovo Way*, authors Gina Qiao and Yolanda Conyers have mapped a course to success for future global leaders."

—Deborah Gillis, President and
CEO, Catalyst

"It was no small feat for a Chinese technology company to purchase IBM's iconic PC division, then to become the #1 PC brand in the world. Through vivid storytelling and filled with practical takeaways, *The Lenovo Way* shows, step by step, how this nimble company has become such a global player—and how their innovative leaders have integrated their diverse workforce into a powerhouse team on the cutting edge of best business practices."

—Dave Duffield, Co-founder and
Chairman of the Board, Workday

"In this book, Gina and Yolanda have captured the essence of high-performing cultures across the world. Such cultures engage the voices and creativity of teams and individuals at all levels. Most importantly, these cultures inspire trust with all stakeholders. I'm a big fan of this wonderful book—and of the authors."

—Stephen M. R. Covey, *New York Times* bestselling author
of *The Speed of Trust* and coauthor of *Smart Trust*

"*The Lenovo Way* illustrates the steps Lenovo has taken to blend both organizational and national cultures. The authors have each played important roles in the events they describe, and they do not hesitate to describe both successes and stumbling blocks Lenovo has encountered along the way. The company is a unique pioneer—a China-based firm that is now also thoroughly global, with a major presence in both advanced economies and emerging markets. Take note of *The Lenovo Way*."

—Dr. Ernest Gundling, President, Aperian Global;
Lecturer, Haas School of Business, University of California
at Berkeley; author of *The 3M Way to Innovation*

"*The Lenovo Way* shows how successfully integrating diverse cultures is crucial to growing a truly global business. When Lenovo purchased IBM's iconic PC business ten years ago, Lenovo's leaders worked with the strengths and best practices of the American team. This book shows leaders and managers of any kind of business—step by step—how prioritizing diversity truly leads to global business growth and success."

—John Haley, CEO, Towers Watson

The Lenovo Way

Managing a Diverse Global Company for Optimal Performance

Gina Qiao and Yolanda Conyers

NEW YORK   CHICAGO   SAN FRANCISCO   ATHENS
LONDON   MADRID   MEXICO CITY   MILAN
NEW DELHI   SINGAPORE   SYDNEY   TORONTO

4 5 6 7 8 9 0   DOC/DOC   1 9 8 7 6 5

ISBN 978-0-07-183724-8
MHID   0-07-183724-8

e-ISBN 978-0-07-183725-5
e-MHID   0-07-183725-6

Library of Congress Cataloging-in-Publication Data

Qiao, Gina.
  The Lenovo way : managing a diverse global company for optimal per-formance/ by Gina Qiao and Yolanda Conyers.
     pages cm
  ISBN 978-0-07-183724-8 (alk. paper) — ISBN 0-07-183724-8 (alk. paper)
1. Lian xiang ji tuan (China) 2. Computer industry—China—History. I. Conyers, Yolanda. II. Title.
  HD9696.2.C64L537 2014
  338.7'62139160951—dc23

                                                          2014020837

McGraw-Hill Education books are available at special quantity dis-counts to use as premiums and sales promotions or for use in corporate training programs. To contact a representative, please visit the Contact Us pages at www.mhprofessional.com.

Contents

Foreword

by Liu Chuanzhi

Founder and former Chairman, Lenovo

On this, the thirtieth anniversary of the founding of our company, I am humbled to be able to present this book, *The Lenovo Way*, to the world. Outside of China, many people still don't know who we are or what we have overcome. They don't know anything about how we achieved the seemingly impossible and became the number one–selling PC brand in the world today.

The answer lies in our people. Our story goes beyond our business to demonstrate just how far a diverse group of people from all corners of the world can come together in mutual understanding if they persist—if the will is there. And who better to talk about our journey of assimilating vastly different cultures than Gina Qiao and Yolanda Conyers, the two executives whose roles in Human Resources cut across all of our key business functions at all levels and who were at the heart of our transition to a truly global enterprise?

Gina and Yolanda are true insiders. Neither of these women was with the company from the very beginning, when we operated out of that dusty old guard shack, but they each played a critical role at a critical point in our rebirth. Both Gina and Yolanda were engaged at the most crucial time in our history, which they write about with such balance and clear-sightedness. Gina, a Chinese woman who grew up in our organization, and Yolanda, an American woman who has experienced Western corporate culture, are a perfect complement. These two women formed a deep friendship, but not without first struggling to understand each other's intentions, keeping an open mind, and, finally, learning and bettering each other. In many ways, Gina and Yolanda are a microcosm of who we at Lenovo are as a culture—and who we strive to be.

Gina is a perfect example of our growth and development trajectory. From modest beginnings, she raised herself to the next level, and then the next. She entered on her own merits, humbly starting at the bottom by working in the secretarial pool. As I recall, her performance in that role was somewhat mediocre. It did not play to her strengths. But her diligence and her willingness to try anything soon distinguished her as one of our most outstanding employees.

Gina is an example of someone who works hard and steadily, and she slowly but surely grabbed my attention. She played an instrumental part in the negotiations for the acquisition of IBM's PC division, and she helped in the early stages of our integration, even going so far as to transfer to our U.S. offices in Raleigh, North Carolina, with her family. She understood how important it was to learn English, to come to grips with a brand-new way of doing things, and to assimilate with the newest members of the Lenovo family.

Yolanda, along with Gina, was instrumental in furthering that integration, blending into our unique culture and helping us to understand, distill, and leverage the best practices of all members of the Lenovo team. I will never forget the day I first met this bright and enthusiastic professional face to face in Raleigh. Things had reached a turning point, and we still had not seen the level of success in defining our true core values that we were looking for. We spoke for hours; I challenged her about all the culture work we had been doing so far, and what struck me was her openness and willingness to dig deep and to get to the roots of the issues. She did not just cling to the easy answers.

During our many subsequent conversations, I learned that Yolanda, like Gina, had come from modest beginnings and had worked her way up through the executive ranks, achieving many milestones as a woman executive and as an African American executive. She achieved academic honors from grade school to graduate school. She was inspired by her father, who had an innate curiosity about other cultures and who took risks, traveling around the world while developing and growing in his line of work, a path that Yolanda herself has followed.

As Gina and Yolanda will both describe on these next pages, our explosion onto the world stage may seem swift to some, and yet nothing about our journey to globalization has been easy. In fact, that was not my vision. In the beginning, all I wanted was to create a small company that could produce something useful for people. When we first started all those years ago, there was no infrastructure, understanding, or support for doing business in China. Where we are today was unimaginable at the time, and, to be honest, I was not that ambitious. I simply wanted to develop my understanding of management philosophy and leverage the strengths of our people.

As agents for American computer brands, we learned from our Western partners. As the Chinese market opened up for businesses like ours, we gradually developed something like a vision—to dominate China's consumer market—and it was only after we achieved that goal that we considered the world beyond. Along the way, we faced many setbacks, but it is in our DNA to persevere and to fight.

Aside from our determination and belief that our goal could be reached, we also developed a very specific methodology. At Lenovo, we use a phasing approach, meaning that whenever we try to approach a target or objective, we try to break down that process into stages, setting benchmarks and targets for each. Before we set targets for individual periods or stages, we think thoroughly about the different links and connections in that process, and we will leave no stone unturned when it comes to the details. Once a target is set, we will spare no efforts in getting to it. And that is how we got here: step by step, thinking, analyzing, and correcting course whenever necessary.

Of course, you have to bring the people with you. All that we are today would not have been possible without the incredible resources of our team. *The Lenovo Way* is, above all, a book about what we are capable of as human beings when we can align behind the same goals. It's a timely lesson, a blueprint for how individuals, businesses, communities, and even governments can move past cultural frictions to gain deeper insights into one another's intentions.

Through our example, we can also show that there is a way for China and the rest of the world to work together and bring together our respective competencies and strengths to achieve a winning scenario. We have heard from leaders of many different countries that they want to work together and that the growth of one economy is beneficial for the health of the other.

Achieving this win-win reality would be good not just for the global economy, but for humankind.

It is up to companies and average people like us to realize this aspiration. Simply put, when we learn how to get along and learn from each other, there are no limits.

Foreword

by Yang Yuanqing
Chairman and CEO, Lenovo

A t Lenovo, we have always taken a unique approach to running our business. Therefore it is appropriate that the authors of this book, Gina Qiao and Yolanda Conyers, are presenting you with a very different kind of business book. *The Lenovo Way* is not the usual how-to manual. Our story of innovation and success is unlike any other, and our globalization journey could not have happened had we followed the rules of a conventional playbook. Instead, what you will find in these next chapters is a series of stories concerning the evolution of our company that focus on how a diverse group of people at Lenovo set aside their egos and their pride to put the interests of the company first, learning how to engage in environments and cultures that were completely unfamiliar to them in order to drive business results.

These are real-life examples of how to build a multinational culture. Many international mergers and acquisitions have not succeeded because their people ultimately failed to adapt. Our willingness to acknowledge what we did not know and start from zero was our secret ingredient. We worked together to set up an entirely new cultural framework that would take us to new heights of achievement.

Personally, I could not be more proud of how far we have come. I joined Lenovo back when it was still called Legend, soon after completing my graduate degree in computer science management at the University of Science and Technology of China in 1989. I had an internship back when we were just a start-up, and I was immediately attracted to the company's vision and energy. In the beginning, I was just the salesperson for foreign-brand workstations and peripherals. Two years later, I was chosen to manage that business. And we grew by 10 times in 2½ years.

Our founder, Chairman Liu, asked me to lead our self-branded PC business in 1994, and we became the number one PC brand in China three years later. Our ability to fully leverage our manufacturing and operations gave us the advantage over international brands, and so did the skills and diligence of our people.

One of those people was Gina Qiao, my neighbor in our company housing complex, whom I used to see every day on the shuttle bus to work. When I ran the PC business at Lenovo, Gina was responsible for PR and marketing in our Home and Education Division. I had heard about some of her pioneering ideas for interacting with customers, her work in creating in-house journals to promote our products, and how well she ran our customer club. I was so impressed with her work that when we merged divisions, I made sure that she was on my team, and this outstanding leader, who is now a member of our Lenovo Executive Committee, has been standing beside me ever since.

After Lenovo began its globalization journey, she was one of the first senior executives to explore the world outside of China. She has lived and worked in Singapore, New York, and Raleigh, working in HR and strategic planning and playing a crucial role as Lenovo created its global culture.

Another asset has been Yolanda Conyers. I first met Yolanda when I interviewed her for the job of our first diversity officer. I was impressed that a world-class veteran executive with more than 15 years' experience was attracted to Lenovo for such an important role. When I asked her how she would define diversity for Lenovo, what struck me about Yolanda's answers was that she was humble. She told me that, although she had previously managed global teams and diversity, she knew that she needed to learn about the Chinese culture and she made a commitment to dive deeply into who we were as a people so that she could help our leadership team come up with the best strategies for East-West integration. I knew immediately that she would be a great fit for Lenovo.

In a story that is parallel to Gina's moving from the East to work in the United States, Yolanda was among the first Western executives to move to China, demonstrating her desire to learn the history of our company and our culture. This move served her well. She began to develop deep relationships in China and to earn the respect of her Eastern colleagues. During her tenure with us, she has been a role model in demonstrating the Lenovo Way, showing ownership and commitment.

Both Gina and Yolanda live up to and embody my requirements for all leaders at Lenovo, including myself: ownership, a learning attitude, and persistence. Ownership means that when you feel like an owner, you do things differently. You put the company first, rather than your own personal interests. You set targets for yourself, rather than being assigned tasks by your boss. And you always try your best to deliver good results, without pressure from anybody else. A learning attitude is a willingness to try new things and new ideas and to practice improving every day. Everyone can learn, be it from books like this, consultants, coaches, colleagues, or competitors—or simply from your own experience.

Through all of this, you need a persistent spirit. It's easy to set ambitious goals, but only a very few succeed in achieving them. Why? Because it is hard to be persistent. When one path is not working, though, always look for another path. That's how you can exceed expectations and go beyond the targets you set.

I often think of this leadership model as a tree: ownership is the root, learning the leaf, and persistence the trunk. If you do all these things, the tree will grow very fast. And now Lenovo has become a tree full of green leaves—new ideas and innovations. Our tree is planted solidly in the ground, with the deep root system of our pride and passion for this company. Its trunk grows tall through persistence and our will to succeed, with branches that span continents across the globe.

The timing could not be more right for this book on many levels. Ten years ago, we transformed Lenovo with a groundbreaking move: the acquisition of IBM's PC division. Since then, we have created one of the world's leading technology companies. That acquisition has clearly been a complete success. Now, we are about to transform the company again with a bold expansion into smartphones and servers through deals that are even bigger than the PC acquisition.

As we undergo an even more monumental transformation in order to adapt and integrate yet more diverse teams, *The Lenovo Way* offers the blueprint, reminding us of what we did right and where we have gone wrong. Looking back and analyzing the past in detail helps us to learn for the future. So read this book and learn how we came this far, so that whatever your industry or enterprise, you can begin to grow your own tree.

Yolanda's Story
Gateway to China

I'd just returned to my home in Austin, Texas, after yet another long-haul flight from Beijing, and I was thrilled to be back in the warm embrace of my husband, Chris, and my two younger sons, Cameron and Colton. The previous three months had been a whirlwind of meetings in Asia that left me in a seemingly permanent state of jet lag. Ever since I first joined Lenovo, I'd been on a steep learning curve that was as exhausting as it was overwhelming. But it was also exhilarating, and I couldn't wait to see what would happen next.

After its acquisition of IBM's PC Division in 2005, it was clear that Lenovo was serious about being a global company. In my entire career, I'd never encountered a more diverse and multicultural group of leaders, and I was inspired. Lenovo was doing its best to walk the talk and become a truly global enterprise.

As the company's first-ever diversity officer—and by the way, Lenovo was the first Chinese company to ever have a diversity officer, much less an African American woman—I had to somehow make this work. I had to figure out how to align everyone behind a common goal while respecting everyone's differences. From language barriers to completely different styles of doing business, we faced enormous challenges before we could even hope to blend seamlessly into one inclusive corporate culture. It was daunting, to be sure, but having learned the value of committing to a job head, heart, and soul, I felt confident.

Or at least, I did until I heard that I was losing favor with my colleagues in China. I quickly called Crystal Arrington, who was then our HR chief of staff, to get more clarity concerning what I had heard.

"Yolanda, what I have heard is that your communication style is offensive. It is too direct and authoritative. Our Chinese colleagues are struggling with you," she said.

That struck me as an odd thing to say. I'd just returned from a trip to Beijing, and the meetings seemed to have gone well. We'd covered a lot of ground, there had been no complaints, and we had seemed to be making some progress. What could possibly have gone wrong in the 24 hours since I'd boarded my plane back to the United States?

I was flabbergasted. We were all still in that getting-to-know-you phase, but I'd always prided myself on my cultural sensitivity. I'd never had this kind of negative feedback before. At Dell, my previous employer, I'd won awards and accolades for my work in leading globally diverse teams. I was the first African American female Dell had hired as a software engineer in product development, and I'd risen through the company's executive ranks based, in large part, on my ability to work with all types of people and get the job done.

Growing up in Port Arthur, Texas, I was raised by a mother and father who taught me to be curious about the world outside our four corners. My dad had worked his way up to be a chief steward on a merchant ship, and spent his life sailing around the world, regaling us with stories whenever he was home on leave. Even as a schoolgirl, when I was bused to an integrated school, I applied this open-mindedness, befriending classmates whose backgrounds were different from my own. I even caught hell for this sometimes when I was hanging out with African American friends. I recalled being accused of "acting white," of communicating "too proper" (meaning with less of my cultural slang), and of being too interested in doing things that people of my color just don't do. My response? I continued on my path, knowing that there was a bigger, broader world out there.

My passion for diversity started very young; it was in my blood. I knew what it was like to be an outsider among my colleagues, and I wanted nothing more than to create a climate in which everyone could feel that he or she had a voice and a place at the table. At Lenovo, we had to mesh a large number of distinct cultural threads together into one strong fabric. The success of the acquisition, and Lenovo's entire future as a global company, depended on this.

However, my Chinese colleagues were viewing me as part of the problem that I'd been hired to fix. Somehow, as I was interviewing all the leaders and staff members one by one, trying to gain an understanding of how everyone would like to work together and to get to the bottom of the many cultural clashes that people were having, I had rubbed people the wrong way.

To back up a bit, Lenovo had been in the process of transforming itself from a completely homogeneous Chinese organization before the 2005 acquisition to a corporate and cultural mosaic, with employees from more than 50 countries, in the space of just two years. After bursting onto the global stage,

Lenovo's top leaders had wisely concluded that the company needed to hire people who had experience in multinational corporations. They needed people who knew how to operate in the overseas markets that Lenovo hoped to conquer in order to enable the company to become a world leader in the high-tech industry.

But the result was three distinct cultures that didn't gel. We called them the "three rivers," referring to Lenovo, IBM, and Dell, the corporate backgrounds of the majority of our employees. We needed to figure out a way to get the three to flow together as one powerful stream. It was bad enough that people outside the company were gunning for us. Therein lay my diversity challenge.

At the time of the acquisition, naysayers predicted failure. There was also some resentment and fear that a Chinese company had acquired an American icon. But the public did not know what we had planned.

Usually, when a foreign company takes over another business, the acquired company gets absorbed into the national culture of the acquirer's headquarters. This isn't always the best way to do things, but it's the easiest way. For years, the Koreans and the Japanese did business according to their own customs, even when they were operating on North American shores. That's how most global companies have operated, with the culture of the company's home base calling all the shots.

Lenovo was trying to do something truly bold. Our chairman at the inception of the acquisition, Yang Yuanqing, insisted on fully integrating all of us. Putting himself at a tactical disadvantage in the short term, he personally dedicated himself to learning both Eastern and Western best practices in business.

The intention was to leverage the strengths and styles from all the cultures—Eastern and Western—to create a world-class global enterprise. Our leaders wanted nothing less than to reconstruct Lenovo's entire cultural DNA. They wanted to create *a new way of thinking* inside one unified Lenovo company.

It was pure genius, and I was relishing the opportunity to try something that had never been done before. This was our chance to be real change agents and prove to the world what could be accomplished in a culture of inclusiveness, compromise, and understanding. Until then, most leaders in my field had focused only on the compliance aspect of diversity: adhering to government regulations concerning demographics and making sure that women and minorities in the workplace felt mentored and had equal employment opportunities.

At Lenovo, we were redefining diversity as something that was much more global and effective as a business strategy. We went beyond the statistical, compliance level of diversity— we wanted to integrate the diverse cultural experiences and points of view of *all* our employees, starting at the very top with our executive committee, to create something trailblazing that would drive business results. This was different, and this was deep.

But at this point, it was all just a little too new. I'd been thrown into the middle of things at a time when everyone— American, European, and Asian—was feeling vulnerable. At various meetings, it was the first time I'd seen white, Western men in the minority. Yet the Chinese employees were feeling overrun by the Western newcomers and by English as the dominant language. We were all out of our element, being forced to question styles of doing business that we'd taken for granted throughout our careers. We all had a new language to learn, and I was no exception.

Outside of various interviews, working groups, and meetings, I hadn't really gotten to know any of my Chinese colleagues on a personal enough level to ask them what the problem was. But Gina Qiao stood out. She hadn't been that forthcoming in the various group settings in which we'd met. In fact, at the first executive committee meeting in Beijing, when McKinsey consultants had shared the results of a cultural audit to identify "strengths and opportunities for improvement" in our new combined work culture, Gina barely spoke. But something told me that she'd be sympathetic. I had also found that the few times we'd talked, she was always very kind, with lots of warmth and sincerity in her smile.

I called to ask her if she'd have dinner with me, and she seemed eager to accept my invitation. We were all staying at the Grand Hyatt Hotel in the Wanchai district of Hong Kong, a spectacular location right on one of the busiest harbors in the world. There was a restaurant on the mezzanine floor of the resplendent marble lobby, with cathedral walls of glass that revealed the surrounding skyline and mountain views. We found a quiet table for two. Gina hadn't been spending that much time in the Beijing office since I'd joined because she was working in Singapore, running HR for the Asia-Pacific region and supporting the president and general manager of Asia-Pacific. But she was beloved and trusted by her colleagues in China, and she was far enough removed from the situation in my department that she could hear both sides without bias. She had a down-to-earth, humble demeanor that belied just how powerful and influential she was within the organization, with a deep knowledge of the Lenovo culture that dated back to the company's earliest years. In retrospect, she was the perfect person from whom to seek advice.

"First of all, Yolanda, I think you are a very nice person," Gina began. "It's obvious to me that you are kind and that your intentions are good. But from what people are telling me, this is not coming across to our Chinese colleagues at all. In fact, they find you too aggressive. They say that you are overbearing and that when you ask them a question, you act as if you already know the answer. You don't listen."

Her words hurt, because they were true. I flashed back to all those conversations that I'd been having with my Chinese colleagues and realized, for the first time, that I'd been the one doing most of the talking. I was so passionate about this work. I had so many ideas about how we would create a new model for global diversity, and I'd been enthusiastically sharing those thoughts with my new colleagues. But I must have come across like a bulldozer.

Gina had plenty of advice to offer, all of it helpful, and I wished I'd heard it earlier. It was the kind of thing that Westerners doing business in China should write down and keep in a wallet for easy reference to help them navigate the complex sensitivities of a culture that is so different from their own—tips that I will share on these next pages. But mostly what I learned was the importance of making face-to-face connections. Relationships, or what the Chinese call *guanxi*, are integral to doing business in the East, but they take work.

I had known how serious relationships are in the Chinese culture, and I had traveled to China once before for my previous employer. But this was truly the first time I had been in a position where the success of my work was heavily dependent on deep cultural understanding. You first have to show up, meet people where they are, be present, and listen.

I told Gina all about my history, explaining that, as an African American and a woman, I had had to fight hard to be heard and to take my place at the table. I wasn't making excuses; I was just trying to help her know what was in my heart and understand my intentions. As we were talking, it dawned on me that the assertiveness that had worked so well for me in the United States had backfired in China because there was no context for it. Most Chinese didn't see me as a black person and a woman; they simply saw me as an American, a foreigner. Not many would have been aware of my ancestors' history of slavery and oppression. Most had no idea. When I told Gina, she was fascinated and eager to learn more.

We talked for hours. By then, it was nighttime, and Hong Kong's legendary harbor was twinkling like a Christmas tree festooned with bright neon lights. As I watched yachts, ferries, and freighters speed by on the busy waterway, it occurred to me that Gina and I could not have picked a more appropriate spot for our conversation. This cosmopolitan territory, a former British colony on the southeastern coast of China, had long been called the Gateway to China, and that's exactly where I was at that point in my life and career.

Together, Gina and I stood on the threshold of momentous change for Lenovo, for ourselves, and for our families. Our budding relationship was the very embodiment of East meets West. There could not have been a more fitting start to our adventure.

Gina's Story

Merging Cultures

When Yolanda first asked me for advice about Chinese culture, I wasn't sure how honest I should be. Although I'd been working out of the office in Singapore, I'd heard the feedback, and I didn't want to upset her. But I also wished that there were someone who could give me advice, because I was having enough of my own problems with my new Western colleagues. So I said to myself, "Why not? Maybe we can both learn something."

Yolanda didn't remember this at the time, but in fact I had interviewed her months earlier, via Skype. She was in Texas, still waiting for the final word about whether she'd gotten the job. I was skeptical, believing that my boss was just trying to hire another person from Dell to keep him company, since that's where he'd come from. I'd never heard of a diversity officer before, and frankly, I thought it was just some nonsense that the Americans had invented as an excuse to bring Yolanda into Lenovo.

I asked my boss not to hire her until I had had a chance to speak with her, and so Yolanda and I set up a Skype chat between Texas and Singapore. On that call, I challenged her about the relevance of a diversity role at Lenovo and mentioned the many obstacles she would face, and I was impressed with each of her responses. She talked about the fact that we had so many different national identities and cultures in our organization from the top down, and that we needed to quickly figure out how to understand, respect, and integrate with each other's ways of doing things. It was exactly what I had been thinking.

After Yolanda joined, our interactions with each other were initially limited. We saw each other at occasional group meetings in Singapore, in Beijing, and in the United States. At a meeting in Beijing, I remember thinking, "Talk, talk, talk. Why do these Americans keep talking when they have nothing to say?" It was an observation about our superiors more than about Yolanda, who was certainly doing more listening than talking on those occasions. But other than exchanging the usual courtesies, it felt as if we were on opposite sides of the table. There was no real communication between Easterners and Westerners. We did not feel like true colleagues.

Most of my work at that time was in Singapore, supporting Lenovo's Asia-Pacific operations, so I wasn't really keeping tabs on my new colleague. As it was, I was too overwhelmed with the tensions and misunderstandings that I was facing. To put it bluntly, I was miserable in that assignment. In fact, it was the lowest point of my life, personally and professionally. I was the only Chinese woman working with a team of mostly Western male executives, and I felt challenged at every turn. It seemed that we had clashing business styles and that I couldn't get anything right.

I wasn't used to being out of my element. I'd spent my entire career at Lenovo, ever since I'd first graduated from college, and I'd been a rising star for the past fifteen years, moving up in the ranks through various departments to the point where I was one of the company's top female executives. As head of the marketing division, I'd won industry accolades, and my concepts had helped drive sales to the point where we had become the dominant PC company in all of China.

I had played a key role in the merger with the IBM PC division, during which time I was responsible for making Lenovo's first global and multinational hires, then helping to integrate our HR systems with those of our IBM counterparts and taking the lead in some of the most delicate negotiations with personnel. So at home in China, where my story was known, I got plenty of respect. But outside China, in strange new places where I was surrounded by foreigners, it was as if I had to prove my worth all over again.

At one point, I was going back and forth with one of my colleagues, an American, for days, trying to make a case about employee performance measures in the region. I felt that he was completely mistaken, and we simply could not agree. I tried speaking with him face-to-face, but it didn't go well. Thinking that maybe my spoken English wasn't strong enough and that I wasn't making myself properly understood, I tried writing down the many reasons why I disagreed with his position, but he still was not persuaded. It was frustrating and puzzling to me that he could not see my point of view, and he must have felt the same way, because no matter how many discussions we had, we could not reach a consensus. So I went to my boss to complain about the situation and lay out the many reasons why I felt that I was right and my counterpart was wrong.

He was not impressed. "Gina, why are you coming to me with this? Work it out between yourselves!" he said.

Bringing problems like this to a boss is the Chinese way, but in the Western style of doing business, it is seen as a sign of weakness. When you are an executive, it is your job to lead and take responsibility, not rely on your superior to fix problems. I know and accept this now, but it was a hard lesson to learn. It was an approach that was fundamentally opposite to the one I'd been used to for the past fifteen years of my career at a Chinese-heritage company.

The list of my missteps in Singapore was long. When I spoke up and made suggestions, they were shot down, yet staying quiet and under the radar was not a solution for me, either. When I was silent in meetings, I was criticized for not sharing.

Later on, as I got to know Yolanda, she taught me a few things about meeting etiquette that helped me a great deal. For example, when the meeting ends and the meeting leader asks, "How does everyone feel? Was it a good meeting?" that is not the time to say no and list all the things you disagree with, because by then the scheduled meeting time is over and everyone wants to move on to the next meeting or project. But back when my English language skills were not so strong, it was all I could do to keep up with the conversation. Invariably, by the time I translated what was being said in English into Chinese, formulated my response in Chinese, and then translated it back into English, the discussion had already moved on, and I'd missed my window of opportunity to speak up. So I had not yet mastered the skills I needed if I was to shine in meetings with Westerners, and this created the impression that either I did not want to offer my opinions or I had no ideas of my own, neither of which was good.

Furthermore, my bluntness did not help the situation. While we Chinese can be sensitive about many things, sometimes we come across as a little too direct in translation. This stems partly from the structure of our language, which conveys information in fewer words, without all the preamble and poetry of English. So when I disagreed with a Western colleague, I would often blurt out, "You are wrong!" and then list the reasons why I thought so. I never meant to hurt anyone's feelings. Only later did I learn the art of Western-style diplomacy, softening the blow with a positive statement before making a sometimes critical point.

As I was adjusting to this new style of communication, I was also undergoing the personal stresses of working overseas, in Singapore, away from my husband, Frank, and my daughter, Georgia, who we decided would be better off at her old school in Beijing. It was a time of personal loneliness and professional frustration.

That's what was going on in my personal and professional life when I met with Yolanda for our heart-to-heart chat over dinner in Hong Kong. So I hardly felt like the all-knowing, wise mentor. And yet I was deeply moved and impressed by her humility in reaching out to me. Yolanda listened carefully, jotting down notes and asking follow-up questions, taking my feedback seriously even though it must have been hard for her to hear.

When she explained her upbringing and her struggles to be heard in the United States as an African American female software engineer in a male-dominated industry, I was surprised. It did not occur to me that an American could feel like an outsider in her own country, and that she had to be aggressive if she was to stand out and be noticed. Yolanda came from a small town in Texas, from a neighborhood where most people looked like her and spoke with a southern accent. Her regional accent had been a problem when she moved to Austin for her first corporate job, and she had taken pains to adjust her speech and manner to the situation, dressing more corporate, deliberately putting herself in unusual situations so that she could learn and grow. As Yolanda talked, it occurred to me that we shared similar stories. I grew up in Dalian, a small provincial town northeast of Beijing, but I went to university in Shanghai, where the accent and dialect were completely different. I, too, felt like a complete outsider. The Chinese have an expression *xiangxiaren*, which means "country girl." It is an insult, and every time I opened my mouth, that's how the Shanghainese viewed me. To them, I was just a common hick from the countryside.

Never in my life have I felt less welcome. Most of the students in my college courses were from other parts of the country, but the Shanghainese lecturers generally ignored the outsiders and taught in Shanghainese, leaving us to figure out for ourselves what they were saying. Even when I tried to get change on the bus, I felt like a foreigner in my own country. When I asked in Mandarin for the price of the bus fare, the conductor kept answering in a Shanghainese dialect that I did not understand. After several attempts to get her to speak to me in our common language, I handed her five renminbi, an amount that I knew was far in excess of what the fare must be, just to avoid the shame of underpaying. When she handed me back the change without even looking at me, I counted out each coin carefully so that I'd know the exact fare the next time and not have to go through this humiliating ordeal again.

In retrospect, the bus conductor probably had no idea how to speak Mandarin, even though it is China's official language. It was not her intention to be cruel. But as a teenage girl living away from home for the first time, I took it as an insult, and I felt the sting of not belonging.

Thinking back to those moments when I felt like an outcast, my respect for Yolanda grew. After all, she was the first HR executive from the United States who had been willing to take an assignment in Beijing, and it took courage. If she could become a role model for others, the whole of Lenovo would benefit.

I promised to spend more time with her when I was in Beijing, to be her sounding board and confidante. Our relationship was only just beginning, but after our conversation, I liked this woman even more. I had a feeling that we were going to become great friends. Although we looked completely different, spoke different languages, and came from opposite sides of the world, we were beginning to see that we had more similarities than differences. Even our work situations were the same, in reverse. We were both fumbling through a completely foreign business culture and trying to fit into a world that we did not fully understand. But at least we understood each other, and I no longer felt quite so alone.

Months later, after I'd moved to Lenovo's U.S. headquarters in Raleigh, North Carolina, I received a package in the mail. It was from Yolanda, and it was a beautiful book of pictures on the American South and slavery. Her intention was to share a little more of her cultural background with me and to give me some deeper insights into this new country where I would be moving with my family. Inside the book cover was a letter in which she described the impact of our first meeting together and how much it meant to her to have me in her corner as both a colleague and a friend.

I was so moved that I had a lump in my throat. Yolanda's book and welcome letter gave me a genuine sense of connection to my new home on the other side of the world. Somehow, by sharing the story of her ancestry with me, she helped me feel as if I belonged.

Our story is a microcosm of the story of Lenovo and its growth on the global stage. On the face of it, we could not have appeared more different, and it's true that the contrasts between East and West in culture, language, and thought processes can be profound. But when we all came together, we found that we had much more in common than we realized. Working side by side toward our common goal made us stronger and better. It wasn't easy, but embracing and blending our international roots has been our distinct competitive advantage in an increasingly global business landscape. We did it not just because we had to but because we wanted to, knowing that it would enrich our lives, both personally and professionally. By taking the time to listen, teach, and understand each other, we broadened our minds and became truly global leaders. We don't just say nice words about cultural diversity; we live it.

That is the Lenovo Way.

CHAPTER 1

Going Global

When Lenovo announced its acquisition of American icon IBM PC (IBM's personal computer division) in 2005, most people predicted the merger would fail. Few could imagine that a business would be able to absorb another business that was three times its size, least of all one that had its headquarters on the other side of the world. Even some of us inside Lenovo had our moments of doubt.

But, over the course of 30 years, we have transformed ourselves from a tiny Chinese company based in a sparsely furnished guard shack on the outskirts of Beijing into a truly global corporation, with 54,000 employees who speak more than 40 languages and live in more than 50 countries. We are not simply a Chinese company, nor are we a typical multinational that's dominated by a single culture. In fact, we have roots in China, the United States, and Europe, with headquarters in Beijing, North Carolina, Paris, and Hong Kong.

Lenovo's strength comes from our diversity. We are really defining what it means to be global. We have a leadership team that is balanced and diverse. Our top 9 executive committee members come from 6 different countries and our top 100 executives come from about 20 different countries. From the top down, our ranks fully reflect the evolving demands, tastes, and needs of our consumers, and that is our great strength.

The story of Lenovo's success must therefore be told through our people and how we wove the many threads of our different cultures together to form a single strong fabric. Among multinationals, the usual model is to grow locally, then export that culture worldwide, but we have grown in multiple regions at once, and this has allowed us to use our global footprint to create a single culture that takes the best from everywhere.

It wasn't easy, but our deep differences and the efforts that we've made to overcome them are the precise reason why we have shot up the charts of the PC industry, reaching the number one spot in July 2013 with 16.7 percent of the global market. At the time this is being written, we've seen 20 consecutive quarters of growth, outpacing the rest of the industry for the past five years, and that's because our leadership has gone to great lengths to embrace a culture of diversity from the ground up. It is an approach that we call the Lenovo Way.

This strategy of balance and diversity cuts across all our business functions. Our team combines many areas of knowledge and expertise, reflecting the diverse tastes and requirements of global IT customers, and that gives us the edge in all our markets.

Moving beyond China's borders was a business decision that our leaders made early on, long before our headline-grabbing acquisition of IBM's PC division (IBM PC), and in this book, you'll learn exactly how we built that road and created a blueprint for a whole new level of globalization, one that is key

> We protect our mature markets and attack our emerging markets; we blend ideas from both East and West; we focus on both consumer and commercial businesses; we focus on PCs, tablets, and smartphones; and we have extended into servers and storage as well as into the cloud with our ecosystem of apps.

for any consumer brand that's seeking to reach its full potential in the international marketplace.

Over these next pages, you'll learn just how bold and prescient our leaders truly were. We took a huge risk and pushed ourselves way beyond our comfort zone. It's the worthy aspiration of many to own a small but manageable business, join the middle class as an entrepreneur, and build the backbone of the local economy—and that's how we at Lenovo began. Then we chose a different path by becoming a global corporation. Those of us who went through the original IBM PC acquisition, transition, and transformation of the business were willing to take a leap into the unknown. We understood that when you are swirling the tail of a phoenix (a mythical bird that represents great possibilities), you can soar.

This book is about much more than a Chinese business operating in the United States or U.S. businesses expanding into China, although the backdrop of Lenovo's unique journey as a business is part of the connective tissue of the narrative. It is about cultural awakenings. Anyone who is or will be operating on the global stage can learn from this book. Its readers can expand their knowledge about cultural dimensions and nuances and what it's like to work in two starkly different environments.

We will include a personalized viewpoint on the creation of a new kind of global company, as we each played our own role in the acquisition and integration of IBM PC and in a number of other major acquisitions since. We will provide our inside perspectives on what this unprecedented transition was like, how it became a catalyst for our own life changes, and the extraordinary adventures that followed for us and our families. After all, globalization isn't just some abstract concept or business strategy—it has a deeply human impact. It transforms lives.

In this post-recession economy, globalization is the favorite buzzword, but all too few walk the talk. Instead, most executives throw the term around without understanding what it really means. So how do lives change, how do families adjust, and how are careers transformed when businesses merge and expand across borders? What does globalization really mean for employees at all levels? How do corporate leaders build a diverse and inclusive culture that shapes best practices in ways that can motivate and inspire their most important resource: their people?

We will answer those questions through our personal and professional experiences, as well as through the stories of our colleagues and our founder and former chairman Liu Chuanzhi. The first chapters will focus on Lenovo's origins as a Chinese company and the pioneers whose courage and persistence helped us conquer the largest and arguably the most challenging consumer market in the world. To understand how far we've come, and the extraordinary nature of the decisions that we made, it's important for you to understand where we began.

Next, we'll detail the steps that we took to acquire an iconic brand and the difficult aftermath of that acquisition as we and our counterparts struggled, not always successfully, to understand each other and blend our cultures. We'll also take you from the transition period following the acquisition of IBM PC to our transformation into the high-tech behemoth that Lenovo is today. In later chapters, you'll also hear from each of us as we break down our HR strategy and tell you how we helped all the moving parts come together into one seamless operation. Because we want you to lose yourself in the chapters to come, we'll include our individual stories, as members of a cast of colorful characters.

Throughout, we'll share takeaways and principles that guided our long journey toward globalization, including:

1. Cultivate a *zero mindset*; past successes don't determine future growth.

2. Leverage the people who are willing to change.

3. Understand that clear communication goes beyond language.

4. Cultural integration is not a sprint; it's a marathon.

Protect and Attack

We'll delve deeply into our Protect and Attack strategy, the development of our core values as a company, and how we execute through our Lenovo Way Five Ps—Plan, Perform,

Prioritize, Practice, and Pioneer—with concrete examples of how we leveraged these principles in our business, whether by streamlining our global supply chains or by developing innovative new products for the post-PC era of our business, making the transition from a core business of PCs to tablets, smartphones, servers, and other mobile Internet devices.

We'll give you all sides of our globalization story, from the integration of our high-tech manufacturing centers to our earliest struggles with basic communication. You'll meet Chinese executives who were so Westernized by their experiences living in the United States that they felt almost foreign when they returned home to Beijing. And you'll hear stories about veteran IBM executives who've formed lifelong friendships with their Eastern counterparts.

Not only does *The Lenovo Way* reflect the big-picture changes in how global businesses operate, but it illuminates the personal challenges of families confronting change, language barriers, and the challenges of moving from isolation to inclusion. It also highlights the dramatic shifts in perspective that women face when we find ourselves learning to navigate high-level careers and high-pressure jobs while simultaneously trying to figure out how to simply survive as wives and mothers in a completely foreign environment, without the usual support networks.

This is also a story about how colleagues can become friends. As longtime high-tech executives, the two of us have mirrored each other in some startling ways that demonstrate just how much people from different cultures have in common when they are willing to dig deep enough.

There will be takeaways, told through engaging and often amusing anecdotes of adjustment and acclimation to new cultures. These tales will capture the before, during, and after of "going global" and the evolution from pat assumptions to complex reality, from isolation to inclusion.

We'll also share the many insights our leaders have gained from analyzing our successes and failures, replaying each move like chess masters. These opportunities for personal and professional dialogue have been a godsend, providing us with essential checks and balances as we navigated our strange new worlds.

This is no ordinary business book because ours is no ordinary business. We've made things happen because we don't cling to conventional business practices. We adapt and adjust to the ever-evolving realities of our global business environment, yet what we do is always based on a set of core values that's become part of our DNA. We live and breathe this stuff, because we believe it is key to the successful future of any global business.

The Lenovo Way is a sweeping book full of urgency about the future of multinational corporations and how we as global business leaders need to conduct ourselves in the world at large. Consider this your official invitation to join us on this expansive ride. In the chapters that follow, you will learn exactly what it's like to dive into the unfamiliar worlds of our colleagues on opposite sides of the earth—and to experience firsthand what it truly means to *go global*.

CHAPTER 2

The Birth of the World's #1 PC Company

Lenovo Principle 1: Great Minds Can Create a Business out of a Vacuum.

Drinking tea together in the business class departure lounge of Raleigh-Durham International Airport, Lenovo executives Gina Qiao and Yolanda Conyers were enjoying a few minutes of downtime, catching up after a whirlwind week of meetings. After months of secrecy and high-level negotiations, Lenovo had just announced two history-making deals: the proposed acquisition of IBM PC's low-end server business for $2.3 billion and the $2.9 billion pact to buy Motorola Mobility from Google.

The two colleagues were preparing to go their separate ways: Gina back to Beijing to meet with senior executives and discuss the impact of these deals on global HR operations, and Yolanda to São Paolo, Brazil, to familiarize herself with the culture and development needs of another recent acquisition, Comércio de Componentes Eletrônicos. Just as they were packing up their tablets and laptops, they overheard a man at the next table say to his friend:

"Say, did you hear about those two huge acquisition announcements this week? What the hell is Lenovo, anyway? Seems like they just came out of nowhere!"

In a sense, it was true. Today we are a global information technology (IT) giant and the number one seller of PCs in the world, but our company began with nothing, born into an economic and technological vacuum with no resources or existing industry to speak of. Looking back, what our founders have achieved seems almost impossible.

It all began in the late fall of 1984, inside a dusty and abandoned guard shack on the northwestern outskirts of Beijing. There was no Silicon Valley to draw from. In fact, there was very little industry to speak of, let alone IT. China's capital, having only recently emerged from the shadows of the Cultural Revolution, was just beginning to open its doors and experiment with free-market enterprise. Back then, Beijing had none of the high-rise buildings, highways, and car traffic that we see today. It was a place still populated by men and women in drab blue-gray Maoist uniforms, going about their business on a silver sea of bicycles. What passed for high-tech was electricity, which was cut by power brownouts almost every day, and maybe switchboard-operated rotary phones.

That was all our 11 founders had when they convened for their first meeting. To house their new business venture, the 11 middle-aged scientists, members of the Institute of Computing Technology under the Chinese Academy of Sciences, were given a deserted guard shack. The gray and red-shuttered building's 300-square-foot concrete interior—the original headquarters of what was to become one of the largest IT companies in the world—was sparsely furnished: there was nothing more than an old pine desk. There was so much dust that the scientists' first order of business was to sweep the floor. A bare lightbulb dangled from the ceiling, lighting the room just enough to reveal a few pegs stuck in the wall to hang ledger books. It fell to Liu Chuanzhi, the youngest member of the group, to scrounge three crude wooden benches so that he and his new colleagues could sit and discuss their next move.

As brilliant as the minds assembled in the austere guard shack were, none of them could have envisioned the Lenovo of today—not even Liu Chuanzhi, the man who would later become known as China's "Godfather of IT." (Years later, in September 2013, *Forbes* magazine would place him first on its "World's Top Leaders and Management Thinkers" list.)

Built on the Ashes of the Cultural Revolution

To understand something of our culture at Lenovo, it is important to know the story of Liu Chuanzhi, our founder and former chairman and the man who built up this global giant from nothing. He was a man with extraordinary vision who saw potential in people and situations that no one else could.

Born in Zhenjiang, a small city in Eastern China, in 1944, Liu Chuanzhi, or Chairman Liu, as we sometimes call him, was the son of a banker who grew up watching his family's fortunes rise and fall in an unstable economy and who barely survived a famine that killed millions of people. A gifted student with aspirations of becoming a fighter pilot, he was refused entry into the air force because a relative had been denounced as a "Rightist," and was sent to study radar technology instead (in those days, students didn't get to choose).[1] It was a fortunate move, as it would eventually lead him into computer technology, although at this time (1962), the field barely existed.

In 1966, just as he was finishing his dissertation, the Cultural Revolution swept the country, and at 22, he joined the first wave of Mao's Red Guards. It was the only option for men of his generation. Anything less than total enthusiasm could have landed him in prison, or worse. But like so many other bright young people in China at that time, Liu Chuanzhi was sincere, caught up in a wave of idealism and nationalism.

As a young man, he had read history and thought deeply about the past and what he could learn from the great writers and thinkers throughout the ages. His curiosity and intellect made him a great student, but his analytical mind also kept him apart from the crowd and destined him to carve out his own path. Of course, it would also make him a target.

In 1968, China's leaders decided that all intellectuals had to be "reeducated" through forced manual labor in the countryside. Liu Chuanzhi was no exception. He was put on a train, sent to a commune in Guangdong Province near Macao, in the far south of the country, and made to plant rice. After a few months of toiling in the fields, he was sent to Hunan Province, where political criminals were forced to do hard labor. He returned to Beijing in April 1970 and learned that many of his friends, including a beloved teacher, had been executed.

Still, it didn't break him. If anything, the experiences of those past few years had strengthened his resolve and taught him a valuable lesson.

> "I learned early on to keep it clean
> and never make mistakes."
> Liu Chuanzhi, founder of Lenovo

"I learned early on to keep it clean and never make mistakes," he shared with us, meaning that by sticking to his path as an engineer and a scientist and never giving in to the temptation to take shortcuts or do anything that even smacked of corruption, he would be doing all he could to protect himself, his family, and his colleagues from repeating recent history.

Despite the hardships he had gone through, Chairman Liu still cared deeply about his country and sought ways to make life better for his fellow citizens. All that suffering never crushed his spirit. Instead, it made him even more determined to have an impact. Little did he know just how much he would be a part of China's extraordinary economic transformation, a true revolution, creating jobs and wealth for thousands and giving many millions of ordinary Chinese access to technology that would improve their quality of life in countless ways.

Playing Catch-Up in the Computer Tech World

Of course, when Liu Chuanzhi finally embarked on his IT career, it wasn't clear that a Lenovo was even possible. China's

"Great Leap Forward" had left it far behind the United States and Japan in terms of computer technology. When our company was started, the economy was centrally planned, and people worked where they were told, whether it was in a factory, on a farm, or in academia. In the early 1970s, as the Cultural Revolution was waning, Liu Chuanzhi and his cofounders were sent to academia, where they worked on developing computer technology for the Chinese government. They were given the task of building a massive mainframe computer that occupied two floors of the Computer Institute building. The project took the best part of a decade and won numerous national awards, yet it served no real purpose. The men, all of them brilliant scientists and engineers, were frustrated and burning with desire to do something that could have real-world applications and improve the lives of the average Chinese.

Observing how the scientists at the academy's various other research institutes were going out and experimenting with various commercial enterprises, Liu Chuanzhi had a vision: to turn all the knowledge and skill that he and his colleagues had accumulated over the years into an actual business. Using his trademark powers of persuasion, he convinced the head of the Chinese Academy of Sciences to give him 200,000 renminbi (about 25,000 U.S. dollars at today's exchange rate) to start the company.

The next order of business was to figure out a way to make money. None of our founders had the least idea about commerce. They had knowledge and a deep set of technological skills, and they shared a vision of bringing computers to the masses, but they still needed to come up with something that they could sell. China's computer industry remained far behind that of the rest of the world, and the country was a long way from making personal computers accessible to the average consumer. So instead we sold our research and our expertise. The company made plenty of mistakes in those early years. "We were mainly scientists and didn't understand the market," Liu Chuanzhi later shared with us. "We just learned by trial and error, which was very interesting—but also very dangerous."[2]

But, year after year, we grew, quickly adapting to the ever-evolving market conditions and regulatory environment. We became agents and distributors for international computer brands like AST, Toshiba, and IBM. Not only did becoming the official agent for these top brands help to keep the business afloat while the company was developing its next breakthrough technology, but the regular contact with foreign suppliers taught us about best practices in Western-style marketing and commerce. It also grew revenues that we could invest in the development of our own brand.

The Birth of a Legend

With that end in mind, we had a secret weapon, a way to make computers accessible to millions of potential Chinese consumers: a Chinese-language motherboard that would enable consumers to use the technology in their own language. While the Roman alphabet has an extremely limited range of pronunciations and uses, Chinese characters, which number in the tens of thousands, are far more complex. But our system had a kind of intelligence, a "linked-thought" feature that automatically came up with a list of possible word compounds that could save the user hours of effort. We called this function *lianxiang*, the Chinese word for intelligence, and this became the new Chinese name of the company (Legend was the anglicized version of our original name). The technology was revolutionary—a breakthrough that no one else had—and the market potential for the product was huge. We were able to insert the motherboards into brands like IBM and eventually to roll out our own, much more affordable products.

Stringing Pearls in the Business World

Liu Chuanzhi was eager to make new hires. He always believed that a company was only as good as its people, and that bringing in bright young professionals would create a new energy and balance the knowledge and experience of the founders with a fresh perspective. For him, the strength of a business has always been a function of the quality of its people and the right mix of diverse opinions and talent, and this big recruitment wave would be the first of many over the next three decades. This is why he has referred to himself as a "stringer of pearls."

His biggest pearl was Yang Yuanqing. Yang Yuanqing's academic credentials at the age of 25 were impeccable. Brilliant and diligent, our future chairman and CEO had received his undergraduate degree from Shanghai's Jiaotong University and his master's from the University of Science and Technology of China. Born and raised in Hefei, Anhui, an industrial town along the Yangtze River in eastern China, "YY," as he is affectionately known by his Lenovo colleagues today, was familiar with a life of struggle. Both of his parents were surgeons, yet they subsisted on the same salary as manual laborers.

Like many others in China's educated class, including Liu Chuanzhi, YY's mother and father were routinely persecuted during the Cultural Revolution. But to them, that was no excuse for anything less than academic excellence from their son. While they wanted him to study to become a doctor, he chose instead to study computer science on the advice of a family friend. In early 1989, he was on track to become a university professor when he accepted a sales position at Legend for about $30 a month. Some of his earliest duties including delivering computers to customers around Beijing. Decades later, he would jet between global business capitals putting together one of the boldest merger and acquisition deals in the history of the industry. Humble beginnings indeed!

Early on, Liu Chuanzhi noticed YY's dedication and integrity. The two men were kindred spirits. This quiet young man was also a deep thinker, yet he got things done, working tirelessly to build up the company's presence in the marketplace. YY, Gina, and so many others who willingly started from the bottom were the leadership of the future.

Growing Beyond China

Growth not only took the form of new hires and increasing revenues but also led to our expansion outside of China, to Hong Kong. Given the licensing laws that existed at the time, there was simply no way that the company would receive permission to manufacture in China. Hong Kong was a hub of free trade where Legend's top engineers could easily get access to all the components and materials that they required for product development.

The time that Legend employees spent in Hong Kong was their first exposure to doing business in an international environment. Although it is geographically a part of China, this small territory on the southeastern coast of China stands apart. Hong Kong natives speak Cantonese, a very different language from Mandarin, but most residents are educated in English and most business is conducted in English. Culturally, Hong Kong is also more Westernized. It serves as an international hub where West and East intersect, and the mindset of the Hong Kong Chinese is very much a blend of the two. It was good practice for our future cultural integration.

The Creation of a Homegrown Brand

Back in China, YY's success at building distribution channels and reselling unprecedented volumes of foreign-brand computers was critical for generating the revenues necessary to fund the company's most cherished dream: to produce its own brand for the Chinese market. The Chinese motherboard was already getting national and international recognition, gaining a lot of press and receiving orders through a technology fair in Hanover, Germany. It was the key component that was making these foreign brands popular, so why not use everything that we had learned to make a Legend computer that could compete on price and reach even more Chinese consumers? By 1990, after six years in business, we'd finally achieved that milestone.

Our first PC was a clumsy-looking device—a basic desktop. But it worked perfectly with our Chinese-language system, and it was a lot more affordable than the imported computers that dominated the market when we launched our first branded product.

But just coming out with a great and affordable computer wasn't enough. Today, everyone talks about China's consumer market as a place of vast potential, with 1.3 billion potential buyers. But, unlike in mature markets such as the United States and Western Europe, getting to these customers is a huge challenge, requiring extensive networks and retail operations that could reach deep into China's hinterlands. In Legend's early days, no one in the IT industry was even attempting to get to these third-, fourth-, and fifth-tier cities, where incomes and infrastructure were far behind those in major cities like Beijing, Shanghai, and Guangzhou. It was too hard. But our leaders knew that this was where we needed to go if we were to become China's leading national technology brand.

To conquer these markets, our chairman had someone specific in mind: YY. He was proving so effective at sales that in 1994, he was appointed head of the personal computer division—the company's core business, or what Chairman Liu would later refer to as "our first battlefield." The challenges of winning over Chinese consumers were immense. Back then, a home personal computer represented two or three months' salary for most families.

Under YY's leadership, we pushed hard into new frontiers. We made sure that the Legend brand was visible and our computers were available, whether they had to be shipped on foot, by bicycle, or on a donkey cart. And since there were not

enough of us to be everywhere, we needed to build great relationships with an extensive network of distributors, giving
them incentives to sell our products by offering them more
rewards for sales and matching sums for advertising.

YY believed in giving everyone a stake, including employees. As we continued to grow, he drastically restructured the
company in a way that would directly reward performance. YY
and the rest of the leadership team were determined to cultivate a spirit of Western-style entrepreneurship, where rewards
were based on hard work and individuals were encouraged to
take the initiative. In addition to the new bonus system, YY implemented employee evaluations, emulating the things he had
learned from his interactions with Western partners over the
years. Suddenly, we had specific job descriptions with clear responsibilities and a system of evaluations that made it clear
who was getting rewarded and why, and what issues needed to
be addressed when targets were not being met. This was a revolutionary concept in the Chinese workplace, and the younger
generation, many of them fresh recruits from graduate school,
thrived under the new pay and performance structure.

Early Strategy: Build a Meritocracy

Gina Qiao was one of those who grew at a rapid pace. Fresh from
an undergraduate management science degree from Shanghai's
prestigious Fudan University, she joined Legend in 1990, right
at the beginning of its first decade of growth as the leading
national technology brand.

Gina's first job was to write procurement letters to various government departments. With her technology and science background, which gave her an intimate knowledge of Legend's computer technology, and her ability to communicate well in Mandarin, she was given the task of writing regular progress reports to the government and explaining why the business needed access to U.S. currency (at the time, the renminbi was nonconvertible) and why we needed to import computer components.

Half a year later, the company decided to try her out in the secretarial pool for the chairman's office. But she lacked a passion for it, so her performance was mixed. When she attended her first formal meeting outside the office, where Chairman Liu was negotiating a deal with the head of a major company, she wore gym shoes.

But the founders of Legend saw potential in this diligent young woman despite her rookie mistakes. She had a work ethic and an attitude—always smiling, trying hard, and never complaining—that caught the eye of Liu Chuanzhi and quickly endeared her to her closest colleagues. Gina didn't always feel that she was best suited to the tasks she was given, but she never refused a request. She was grateful to have a spot in one of China's up-and-coming IT businesses, and she took nothing for granted.

She was also relieved to have a place to live. As a recent university graduate, she couldn't afford housing, as was the case for many who were coming to work for Legend at the time. For the first year, Gina lived in the company dorm, where she slept on a bunk bed in a small room that she shared with three other female employees, including Alice Li, our future colleague in human resources. It was a humble beginning, but she never felt more at home.

Build Incentives to Achieve a Loyal Workforce

Not only did Gina feel at home, but the company actually gave her, and 71 other employees, a home. In 1992, Legend built three 6-floor apartment buildings in a northern suburb of Beijing, above the Fourth Ring Road that runs around the city, in an area surrounded by empty fields. Most state-owned firms gave their employees incentives by giving them a company apartment, but it could take up to 20 years for an employee to get one, if he or she could get one at all. Legend decided that employees should pay for their own apartments rather than being given one—another form of incentive. But since it was next to impossible for any young graduate to get a mortgage in those days, Legend became, in effect, a property developer and mortgage lender.

Each employee who signed up for the deal agreed to pay for the apartments in monthly installments of about $50 a month, which were taken from their salaries. Many employees worried that they would not have enough left over for other living expenses. Gina, who was still just a secretary, almost didn't make the list, and when she did, she felt as if she'd won the lottery. After living in a bunk bed, the 600-square-foot accommodations seemed positively palatial. This privilege in a city where housing was scarce made Gina love the company even more.

One of her neighbors in the company apartments was YY, who lived in the building opposite hers. Gina didn't really know him to talk to, because he was working in a different department at the time, but she used to notice him on the bus during their daily commute to work, when he would be reading through a stack of papers. While everyone else on the bus gossiped and laughed, all he did was read. Gina was intrigued by this quiet, studious man who seemed so focused on business, even outside the office. Back then, in 1993, this kind of intensity seemed strange to Gina, who was just coming off of maternity leave after her daughter Georgia was born and was focused on other things besides work. That passion and drive had yet to kick in.

Gina's career at Legend hit a turning point in 1995. Previously, Legend had had two different sales departments: commercial and consumer. They were almost like two different companies, and they rarely interacted. At that point, Gina's job was to market home computers to families, students, and schools. Gina's consumer division wasn't bringing in anything close to the sales in YY's commercial unit, so the two departments combined, requiring Gina to take a more junior position.

But she didn't complain. Instead, she humbly accepted her new role, put her head down, and worked hard, and she soon was noticed by YY.

What Gina didn't realize at the time was that YY saw her as a star employee who was well worth cultivating. His acknowledgment of Gina's abilities notwithstanding, he pushed her hard, insisting that she stay late and put in more hours. Their working styles were completely different: she was 9 to 5, and he was around the clock. (A great deal has changed over the past

20 years.) But he tended to be hardest on those who had the greatest potential.

> "I thought that if you can't get it done in the
> eight hours, you are not doing your job properly.
> I've changed so much over the past 20 years!"
> —Gina

YY could see that Gina's particular skill was coming up with a message, packaging it creatively, and aiming it with precision at its target audience. In the past, most ads had taken the form of wordy, government-style slogans. They were dry and informational at best. But by the early nineties, the advertising industry, especially in dealing with the IT industry, was getting increasingly sophisticated. Billboards were everywhere, and companies needed to find ingenious new ways of establishing themselves in the public consciousness. Legend had increased its ad spending year after year, in lockstep with the need to stand out from the competition. The computer industry was starting to hire ad agencies; develop television, print, and billboard advertising campaigns; and leverage media relations.

The Rise of a Marketing Star

Gina's most memorable campaigns in the 1990s included the celebration of Legend's millionth PC, in 1998, in which she and her team designed a ceremony attended by Intel chairman

Andy Grove, who took a Tianqin 959 PC for the Intel museum's permanent collection. It was a way of saying that Legend, and China's PC industry in general, was emerging as a global force.

But perhaps Gina's most powerful promotion was introducing the Tianxi or Millennium computer—Legend's pioneering Internet computer with a "one-touch-to-the-Net" feature—which was launched in 1999 to celebrate the coming of the new century. At that time, the Internet was only just becoming popular in China. Most users were still relying on dial-up connections that required special permission and passwords to get online, but Legend's development team knew that this would soon change, so they designed the Tianxi computer to eliminate that hassle. Gina knew that this would be big, and it was. Her launch event in Beijing created a huge amount of buzz among consumers and throughout the industry.

For Gina, every market milestone, and there were many, was a thrill ride. Her marketing wins worked in tandem with the small but nimble sales team that was making major inroads into China's provinces under YY's leadership. At first, we had been using direct sales and a network of distributors. But YY gave up on this approach in favor of exclusively using independent agents to avoid the costs of administering a complex sales network. The key to making this work was building relationships with the distribution agents based on trust. This was how we distinguished ourselves from competing foreign brands, many of which tried to squeeze distributors' margins. These moves, combined with our superior after-sales service, ensured our place as the market leader by a wide margin.

What to Do When
Market Share Erodes

But then sales started eroding. After such steady growth, it came as a shock to us to see our position slipping so fast. That happened because Dell had entered China's market, throwing all its resources into competing for our biggest customers. Up until that point, foreign competition had not been an issue for Legend, because those brands were priced beyond the reach of most mainland computer buyers, and few of them had awakened to the fact of China's huge potential outside the main cities. We had the benefit of both local knowledge and lower costs, so Dell's wins were confusing to us.

After some study, we figured out that the problem was the distribution-based model. The technique that had been so effective in conquering China's vast territory was now leaving us vulnerable to a sneak attack. Market conditions had changed, and for a moment we had failed to realize this fact. When Dell, which was conducting direct sales, won over one of our big commercial clients, such as a bank or a large state-owned enterprise, our distributors were under no obligation to tell us about this. We needed to learn all we could about Dell's direct sales business model so that we could beat it at its own game.

So YY formed a task force with his most talented sales executives, including Liu Jun, our current EVP in charge of the Mobile Business Group, and Chen Xudong, now SVP for China and Asia-Pacific Emerging Markets, who was in charge of quality control at the time. Together, the team discovered that we needed to employ two models for PC sales: the transactional model for ordinary consumers and small-to-medium-sized enterprises, and the relationship-based model for large accounts, like major banks and institutions.

We'll talk more about these two models, and Liu Jun's role in perfecting them, in a later chapter. But, simply put, the transactional model focuses on speed. Instead of catering to the customer and trying to build a long-term relationship, the transactional model, also known as the "push model," pushes products to customers, setting trends and dictating what the market needs. The relationship or "pull" model, on the other hand, caters to the large-enterprise customer, tailoring product development to the customer's specifications in hopes of receiving huge orders and repeat business.

After our wake-up call from Dell, we made it our business to understand what we did not know. Eventually, we reached a level of excellence in both models, at least in the Chinese market, but it was a steep learning curve.

. . . .

When you and another chicken are the same size,
the other one will always think you are smaller than
he is. When you are a rooster and the other guy is a
little chicken, you might think you are pretty big,
but the other guy thinks you are about the same size.
Only when you are an ostrich will others admit you
are bigger. Be careful not to overestimate yourself.[3]
—Liu Chuanzhi

. . . .

Toward the end of the millennium, we'd had so much success and grown so fast that we took what we'd achieved for granted. In an ever-evolving IT industry, that kind of complacency can be deadly. You have to stay humble, because the moment you think you're at the top, you can fall right back to the bottom. Sustained success can't happen without that entry-level attitude, that willingness to work as if there is always something to prove.

This wasn't the last time that Dell would be a threat. Its cheaply priced computers and aggressive direct sales approach in China meant that it was always biting at our heels. But at least, now we knew. We still had a lot to learn and a long way to go, and there would be many more errors along the way. But we never made that particular mistake again.

Lenovo Strategy Takeaways

- When you start with nothing, there are no limits.

- Be a stringer of pearls: assemble the best minds in the right positions for maximum growth.

- Take the business to your customers, even by donkey cart.

- Don't grow so tall that you miss what's happening right at your feet.

- Adapt your sales strategy to fit all customers, big or small.

Do What We Say, Own What We Do

In March 2010, in Vienna, our founder, Liu Chuanzhi, known as Chairman Liu, delivered a speech to introduce our groundbreaking Lenovo Way strategy, which you will read more about later in the book. Here is an excerpt from his speech, which eloquently and succinctly describes who we at Lenovo are.

....

As the saying goes, the good shepherd lays down his life for the sheep, but a hired hand abandons the sheep and runs away when he sees the wolf. In the same way, a built-to-last company must have true owners instead of only hired individual contributors, because only owners will treat the company as their own business, and will put the company's interests first rather than treating it as a way of earning their bread.

Of course, the company will reward those who can be true owners with commensurate returns and long-term incentives. In addition to owners, a built-to-last company also needs a multitude of highly motivated employees with entrepreneurial spirit. These employees have the following attributes:

- The intention to improve themselves continuously (day after day, year after year)

- Ambition, setting higher and higher goals

- An ability to learn and summarize from past experiences

- An ability to adapt to constantly changing environments with proactive innovations

- A desire to work hard and to strive to turn a 5 percent possibility into a 100 percent reality

- Self-motivation—working like an engine to drive others rather than like a gear being driven

In return for the huge contributions that these employees make, the company will provide them with good compensation and benefits, career platforms, and space for growth. They can make full use of their talents and add value to their personal brands.

But the company won't allow those who lack a sense of responsibility to stay and won't promote those who lack motivation for betterment. For those in managerial positions, it is not enough for them to say that they have a sense of responsibility. They've got to have ideas, initiative, and ambitions.

Comments and suggestions should be presented in an open, straight way. If they are, the atmosphere of the company will be constructive, and comments and suggestions are meant to help the company.

So how do we bring this culture to life? I like one of the quotes that was put in our office in Raleigh:

"Leading by example is not the important way to inspire people, but the *only* way."

The key to bringing a culture to life is whether managers at different levels can live it and exemplify it, and especially whether senior executives can practice it and set an example for subordinates. Only when leaders at all levels really believe in it, work on it, do it, and change their behavior can trust be established and employees be convinced. Then the transformation of employees' routine behavior and the transformation of the company's culture will take place. To bring culture to life, we need to work on these areas:

- Leaders at all levels must be the advocates of the new culture by communicating and promoting, repeatedly, what we want to stick to. They must be the role models by living and practicing the new culture. The words and actions of leaders will shape the direction of the company's culture and will determine the credibility of that culture. A leader must lead and guide his team in reviewing and summarizing best practices and codes of conduct to learn, apply, promote, and duplicate, and to do things right. It is necessary to apply and incorporate culture into management, so that the culture will be tested by and nurtured in business operations.

- Culture should be institutionalized, especially in systems tied to the screening, recruiting, and promotion of talents. A culture index, as an important element of assessing and promoting talents, should be incorporated into key performance indicators.

Of course, this requires a solid framework, based on three management keys:

1. Set up the right leadership team. This includes structure, governance, and the roles and responsibilities of each member, with the members being developed and guided

through discipline, rewards, and recognition. They must approach the business as entrepreneurs and owners of Lenovo.

2. **Define the strategy.** We need to have a vision, with clear goals and objectives. Simply stating our vision is not enough. There has to be a road map for achieving our goals, including key performance indicators for the year, and reviews and measures for the achievement of these goals.

3. **Last but not least, take people with you.** This happens through building a shared culture and enabling the entire organization, equipping people so that they are able to fight for our goals in the right way, in a structured way.

CHAPTER 3

Managing a Corporate Culture Clash

Lenovo Principle 2: Stretch beyond your comfort zone for maximum growth.

Dazed from the 14-hour flight from Beijing to New York's John F. Kennedy Airport, Gina had no idea what to make of the aggressive and impatient man who was interrogating her at U.S. Immigration. At most, she had an English vocabulary of about 100 words, and she found even the simplest of questions baffling.

"Did you come to the United States for work?" he asked her.

Struggling to remember the few words of English that she'd memorized before her trip, Gina explained that she'd flown in for business and that she represented Lenovo, the company that had just acquired IBM PC.

"What? You own IBM? A Chinese company I have never heard of? How is that possible?" the immigration officer asked her.

Gina took his angry demeanor to mean that he didn't believe that this petite, soft-spoken woman with broken English could possibly be part of a company that was taking over an American icon. She had no idea that this gruff manner was business as usual in JFK's immigration hall, particularly at the end of a long shift spent processing passengers from multiple long-haul flights who spoke a wide variety of languages and made multiple mistakes in filling out visa forms. (Years later, these border crossings would usually end up with a friendly chat.)

Gina's head was throbbing, her ankles were swollen, and all she wanted was to get to her hotel room to shower, make some calls to her office back in Beijing, and sleep. There were going to be some big meetings the next day, and she wanted to be at her best. Just as she was about to give up hope, and fearing that she'd be turned around and put back on a plane to China, the irritated border official stamped her passport and waved her through.

It was Gina's first time in New York on her own, and it was certainly not the kind of reception she was accustomed to when traveling for business around China, where she was often greeted by colleagues the moment she stepped off the plane. On this trip, she was left to fend for herself. There was no one to meet her, just the driver of an airport taxi whom the assistant in the Lenovo offices had hired—a man with a thick Bronx accent and an attitude that made the immigration officer seem positively jolly.

"So where to, ma'am? Are you going to White Plains?"

Gina had no idea what he was talking about. The address she had been given didn't specifically mention White Plains, a place that she'd never heard of. Lenovo's U.S. offices were in Purchase, not far from there, but she wasn't familiar with the local geography. She pulled out the only information she had and stammered out the address, pronouncing the words as best she could. Clearly, the driver did not understand.

"White Plains! *White Plains!* That's where you're going, isn't it, lady?"

This exchange continued for a while, and the driver was getting impatient. The less Gina seemed to understand, the louder he got, as if she must be slightly deaf. Still parked by the terminal, they were holding up traffic, and Gina feared that he was about to kick her out when he called Lenovo's office to confirm her destination.

He passed the phone to Gina and, much to her relief, there was a Mandarin-speaking Lenovo assistant on the other end of the line. The woman explained to Gina that White Plains was the name of the area where she was staying, and the car finally started to move. Although another crisis had been averted, Gina was stunned at the harshness of the encounter and at how easily a simple miscommunication can create such a scene.

This hard landing took place in October 2005, shortly after Lenovo's headline-grabbing acquisition of an American icon, IBM's PC division, had been made official. Until then, Lenovo could hardly have been described as a global player. In fact, no Chinese company could have made that claim. In the lead-up to the acquisition, many of us had been asking ourselves how we could possibly acquire one of the world's most iconic brands, with revenues many times our own.

Internally and externally, people were bewildered by the move. But it was genius. After spending the last five years trying and failing to break into overseas markets, what better way of becoming a global company could there be than by acquiring the biggest and most iconic brand in the industry? Chairman Liu and YY knew that the only truly effective and immediate way to grow globally would be to acquire a multinational technology company. With no international brand presence, much less experience, growing into a multinational company organically, country by country, could have taken decades. An acquisition was the fast track.

It was time for us to stretch ourselves. We knew that this would not be easy, but we had to be willing to take on tasks with which we were completely unfamiliar (like Gina's first venture on her own to New York), risking embarrassment and sometimes failure, to learn all we could about the next frontier of business. In order to accelerate our growth rate, we needed to tap new markets far beyond our borders. We had already conquered the Chinese market. Our position as the market leader in PC sales was well established. But our future was in the rest of the world, in markets and territories that were completely alien to most of us.

The Long-Term Lenovo Strategy Emerges

In 2000, at the turn of the millennium, our leaders outlined a new mission, anticipating the kind of company that we wanted to become decades into the future: a high-tech, service-oriented, and global company.

At that point, we had taken no major actions toward these goals, but that was the dream. We knew that there was a wide gap between where we were and what we needed to become. And yet, on many levels, we'd already been preparing for this moment in our history for more than a decade. Incorporating in Hong Kong was the first in a long series of steps toward becoming an international company. The next was our listing on the Hong Kong Stock Exchange. Each of these major steps brought us closer to the brink of globalization. But our progress had been slow, steady, and deliberate.

Liu Chuanzhi had always played the long game. Everything was thought out and planned years ahead of time. While we spent most of the nineties developing new products and pushing them in markets all over China, we were also working hard to establish our presence within the international financial community. To that end, in 1990, Liu Chuanzhi hired Mary Ma, who was educated at King's College, London, before taking a position as department director of his usual poaching ground for senior leaders—the Chinese Academy of Sciences.

He put her in charge of all Hong Kong operations, from strategic investment, financial management, and corporate marketing to overseas business development. She also ran operations in Hong Kong, including manufacturing of the motherboards and other components. It was a shrewd hire. Liu Chuanzhi proved once again that he could spot the pearl and put her in exactly the right position. Mary was the type of executive who inspired confidence in her international counterparts, and she was just the kind of face our chairman wanted to present to the world. She has since retired from Lenovo and now holds a position on our board, but her distinguished career as our CFO, among other top finance positions she's held, has earned her recognition as a leading executive in *Forbes*, *Fortune*, and *FinanceAsia*.

Early Exposure: Lenovo's IPO

The result was a highly successful IPO in February 1994—one of the first listings of a major mainland Chinese company on the Hong Kong Stock Exchange. Our debut on the world financial stage was so eagerly anticipated that we became heavily oversubscribed, raising close to $30 million. Analysts heaped praise on Legend for solid management, strong brand recognition, and plenty of potential for further growth, causing the stock price to hit a high of HK$2.07 (USD 0.27) on its first day of trading.

Raising money wasn't going to make our globalization happen in and of itself. Although we knew that, since we had more than 27.5 percent market share in China, the next step had to involve moving into overseas markets if we wanted to continue our growth story, we had little or no experience beyond the borders of China and Hong Kong.

Most of our knowledge of Western-style business practice came from our early distribution partnerships with companies including IBM, but our information was secondhand. Yes, we were no longer just a domestic Chinese play. By 2002, we were actually among the five bestselling computer manufacturers in the world, but what did that really mean? Although we'd been making inroads into the Asia-Pacific region, where we'd become the leading PC vendor by 1999, our market share beyond the region was still less than 1 percent. We said that we wanted to go global, but we didn't even understand what that meant.

Opening branches outside China was just one of several things that we were trying in order to diversify, including branching out from our core PC business and becoming a provider of Internet and other high-tech services, as well as developing a communications business. We didn't realize at the time that making and selling computers is a very different business from providing Internet services, so these strategies had mixed results. Overall, we were too scattered, and we weren't as profitable as we could have been. Meanwhile, foreign computer companies, affected by slowing business in their local markets, took another look at China, with Hewlett-Packard and Dell becoming increasingly aggressive in their quest to attract more Chinese consumers. This hurt our core business, PCs.

Part of the problem was that many of us had been so busy growing the business that we hadn't taken the time to look up at the horizon and see the road ahead. We were managing the business while we were learning. We had to adapt quickly to new roles, and when we found issues, we would look for solutions on a day-to-day basis.

Stripping Down to Core Competencies

By March 2003, the solution was to strip the business back down to our core competencies: the development, manufacturing, and marketing of PCs, focusing solely on globalization as the next major step. But we needed the right people, and that was where Gina came in.

When Gina first took on the role of head of HR in 2002, it wasn't even clear to her what exact function of the business human resources was. It seemed to her that it was solely a back-office administrative function, kept separate from the rest of the business, that handled payroll and hiring at most. When she was first approached in 1999, she didn't even want the job. But YY pressed her again, three years later, as the need to attract talent with multinational experience became more urgent.

Gina still didn't understand why they would want to take her away from marketing, a role at which she excelled, and she could not think of any areas with more impact on the company's bottom line. But she knew YY well enough by then to understand that it was part of an overall strategic vision, and that some deep thinking had already gone into his decision. She also recognized that the next step for the company was going global and recognized how sorely we were lacking in international experience.

Despite the challenges, YY's thinking was well ahead of its time. They realized that as more Chinese companies turned to global markets, the competition for talent would be fierce, and that they needed one of their top executives in the job. But the HR field in China was so nascent in the early 2000s that you could count on one hand the number of Chinese HR executives with multinational experience. With no HR courses or seminars to attend, Gina made it her business to find out who were the best and either hire them or bring them in as consultants.

What information there was about this burgeoning field Gina absorbed like a sponge, taking courses, reading books, and bringing in a steady stream of HR professionals and executives from IBM, McKinsey, Intel, Siemens, and Lucent

Technologies to conduct seminars for her team. She had to find different talent for multiple business groups at the most senior levels. She transformed the way Lenovo hired, focusing more on senior, experienced professionals instead of just the bright young university graduates the company usually hired and groomed from junior-level positions. She implemented top-level training programs, and she scoured the country and the globe for English speakers with multinational experience.

There were a few, but there were none at the top leadership level. Most of the people available were young and had studied overseas but had yet to reach higher than the vice president level in their careers. They either lacked experience in the industry or hadn't been in the workforce long enough to be more than middle or junior management. What she needed most was global leaders, but they were hard to attract. Most of them preferred to work at an established multinational or to go overseas. They didn't believe that a Chinese heritage company was serious about becoming international.

The Importance of Branding:
A New Look

In addition to finding global talent, a major rebranding would help us in our preparation to go global. Still wearing her marketing hat, Gina helped to spearhead our name change in 2003. After some careful research, we realized that our English name, Legend, was far too common outside China's borders. Not only could that lead to potential problems with name use restrictions overseas, but it did not say anything unique about the brand.

For the China market, we kept the Chinese name, *Lianxiang*, or "connected thinking," a name that had been resonating well in the mainland market. For overseas markets, however, we came up with Lenovo, a combination of the first part of Legend, *Le*, and *novo*, which is Latin for "new," referring to innovation and expressing the same idea in several languages. It was a way of keeping our original core and at the same time indicating that we were all about evolving and moving forward.

To ensure that the message was firmly established in the minds of the Chinese public, Lenovo invested in advertising and promotion, including giant billboards and ads on CCTV—China Central Television—during the peak postnews broadcast time slot. The television ad, which ran every day for eight weeks, showed the old Legend sign disappearing into the water and the new *Lianxiang*/Lenovo logo rising like the sun. Another ad, which coincided with the news coverage of China's first manned spacecraft mission, featured the word "Lenovo" floating in the atmosphere, with the tagline "Transcending depends on how you think."[1]

Don't Acquire Before It's Time, but Be Ready to Grow

Coincidentally, the opportunity for a deal with IBM PC first arose at about the same time as we began our rebranding. But when we were approached by the company in early 2003, we did some risk analysis, and Liu Chuanzhi decided against it. The timing wasn't right. Our former chairman questioned whether we had the capacity to manage such a major transition. Even though we were number one in the Chinese market, and had been for several years, our leaders recognized how much we did not know and worried about their lack of experience in running a global company. There was a lot of self-questioning and intense internal debates in the two-year period leading up to the decision. The Chinese media would later call the deal "the snake that swallowed the elephant," and our leaders were well aware that a move like this could either make or break us.

Culturally, especially, we weren't sure if we were ready. Since the late 1990s, after learning and observing the practices of our global partners, YY had been doing his best to establish a more Western tone and management style. In the past, we'd had a much more disciplined and military approach to running things. Liu Chuanzhi had created a rule, for example, that people who arrived late to meetings had to stand in front of the group to demonstrate the importance of being on time. One of his earliest efforts to Westernize, in 1997, took place when Legend relocated to a new building. YY insisted that employees dress in a more professional manner, wearing jackets and ties. He also had the staff members trained in phone etiquette. It was part of his overall plan to have Legend employees think, act, and feel like professionals in a multinational company. His next move was to change the way employees addressed their superiors. In a typical Eastern-style business practice, leaders would be referred to by their name and titles. Gina would have been addressed as "Senior Vice President Qiao" or, in Mandarin, *Qiao Zong*, and YY's honorific would have been "Chief Executive Officer Yang," or *Yang Zong*. YY decided to do away with this formality altogether and stick with given names to foster a more collegial atmosphere and create the sense that we were not hierarchical, that we were equal.

It was a hard sell. At first, Legend employees were so afraid of being disrespectful that they didn't address their superiors by name at all. It was hard to change the habit of a lifetime. In Eastern culture, respect for superiors and elders is ingrained from birth. The staff members felt awkward and embarrassed. Frustrated, members of the project committee issued a memo, threatening employees with fines if they accidentally addressed their bosses by their more formal titles.

For the next week, YY had the members of our top management line up to greet employees in the main lobby, as they were arriving at work. Each executive wore a name tag with the words, "Hello, my name is _____." They shook hands and introduced themselves to each of hundreds of employees as they walked in. It was an exhausting process, but it did the trick— yet another example of how determined Lenovo, under YY's leadership, could be in carrying out a plan. Even if it took several attempts, they always found a way, whether it was changing the culture or selling a multimedia PC to villagers in Inner Mongolia.

Years later, YY would be praised in an *Economist* article for transforming the company's culture from "wait and see what the emperor wants" to a much more egalitarian, welcoming environment for colleagues from the West.[2] But this was just the beginning of a process that was to take years. These were small steps toward adapting to a more international, Western-style business environment, and the monumental effort that they took highlighted just how far we had to go. That's why Liu

Chuanzhi and Legend's board of directors were so concerned about the viability of the possible merger with IBM PC.

But YY was passionately in favor of the deal and persisted in pushing the idea for a year before Liu Chuanzhi finally relented and agreed to hire McKinsey and Goldman Sachs to do an analysis of the financials and find out exactly what would be required to make such a merger work.

Leverage the Employees Who Are Ready for Change

First, there were exploratory talks with Lenovo's IBM PC division counterparts. Peter Hortensius, our present-day chief technology officer and senior vice president of research and technology, was running the product division of IBM's PC business at the time. He was all for the acquisition, because he knew that IBM was no longer interested in the PC product side of the business.

Peter was among the first to meet with Lenovo executives, including Mary Ma and George He, who was our chief technology officer in 2003. Their contact was brief, but he had a good feeling. Later, on April 1, 2004, he met with our key leaders— George, who is currently our SVP of ecosystem and cloud services, Mary, YY, and others—on his home ground at the Sienna Hotel in Chapel Hill, North Carolina. The talks were stop and start, through a translator, but over the course of the three-day meeting, he could sense how earnest our key people were and how hard they were trying to figure out how to move forward with the deal.

I was curious about how this would work. Lenovo was looking to buy a business three times its size; it was determined to go global, but had very little global experience. It was seeking to take on a business that was frankly, from a PC perspective, the mirror image of who it was: very local, with an incredibly strong market share, but only in one market, and mostly desktop. IBM was more notebook-, global-, and large business–oriented as opposed to the individual consumer. On the one hand, that was great—very complementary and not a lot of overlap. But on the other hand, wow. I had to ask myself, "How much do they understand of our business and what are they really interested in?"

—Peter Hortensius

Fu Pan: Self-Critique for Success

That was also what Lenovo's leaders were trying to figure out. When the consultants had completed their deal assessment, on April 20, 2004, our top executives met at Legend Holdings' headquarters in Beijing to thrash out the idea amongst themselves. They conducted what we at Lenovo later called a *Fu Pan* (Chinese for a thorough accounting of the successes and failures of a business move), meeting in secret in a top floor conference room to interrogate each other about the potential pitfalls. Our chairman and board of directors grilled Mary, YY, and the McKinsey and Goldman Sachs consultants about whether or not Lenovo's management was truly capable of running such a large and complex business after the merger. An article that ran in *BusinessWeek* at the time aptly described the meeting as tense, like a trial in a courtroom. And, after three days, they reached a verdict: yes, it could work, if we could bring in IBM's top executives to help run the business.[3]

In the end, our leaders believed that the benefits outweighed the risks. With Dell continually nipping at our heels in China, joining forces with IBM PC would balance us in all the areas where we were lacking. We were a perfect complement for each other. At Lenovo, we specialized in PCs for the consumer market, and we were able to produce high-quality products cheaply and efficiently. IBM was winding down its consumer PC business, focusing instead on commercial sales to large businesses and enterprises. Its massive sales force of 10,000 people covering 60 countries and its vast international network of 9,000 business partners could grow our global market share and get our own branded PCs into the hands of millions more consumers outside of Asia, the only area where we were dominant. Our strengths did not compete with each other, so, on multiple levels, it was the ideal arranged marriage.

The decision to go ahead with the purchase of IBM PC was the beginning of months more negotiation between the two parties. The rest, the details, was up to leaders like Gina to negotiate. She felt handicapped not just by the language barrier, but by the completely different style and etiquette.

Make No Assumptions When Dealing with Different Cultures

Going into her first face-to-face meeting with her American counterparts, she'd expected them to be friendly, open, and not especially sophisticated. By the end of the meeting, she felt as if she'd just been through an intense battle and come out of it bloody and bruised. The object was to try to retain IBM PC's best talent and give them incentives to help Lenovo manage the transition after the acquisition was made. But those on the American side did not seem prepared to give or compromise on any of the compensation and benefit terms. They seemed brash, confident, and determined to squeeze all they could out of the deal.

When one of the women at the meeting leaned back in her chair, put her arms behind her head, and put her feet up on the table, Gina was offended. What was a commonplace, relaxed pose in the United States, especially in the engineering field, where people are less formal, signaled blatant disrespect to Gina, who came from a culture where you sit up straight in meetings, with your hands folded on the table. When there is a language barrier, that kind of body language takes on even more significance as a nonverbal cue. She later realized that body language does not have the same connotations in the U.S. as it does in China. But achieving that level of understanding took time.

The Announcement That Rocked the Business World

After months of back-and-forth negotiations, Lenovo announced the acquisition on December 8, 2004. Because of politics and the suspicion aroused by a Chinese company taking over the personal computing division of an iconic American brand, it was another five months before the U.S. government approved the transaction, on May 1, 2005. Lenovo paid IBM $1.25 billion, approximately $650 million in cash and $600 million in Lenovo Group common shares. IBM thus became a shareholder, receiving 18.9 percent of Lenovo's shares, a percentage that it would reduce over time. Lenovo also assumed $500 million of IBM's balance sheet debt.

The terms of the deal were beneficial to both sides. It created, in Lenovo, the third-largest personal computing company in the world, with approximately $13 billion in revenues, annual product volume of roughly 14 million units, and, at the time, about a 7 percent market share in the global PC market. The agreement also established a broad-based alliance between IBM and Lenovo Group, allowing IBM to continue to provide end-to-end solutions for its clients, with Lenovo being the preferred provider of IBM-branded personal computers for IBM's existing clients, while IBM continued to provide financing and maintenance services for its PCs.

In terms of revenues, the deal effectively quadrupled Lenovo's size overnight. The deal also gave us the Think brand, including the iconic ThinkPad notebook, IBM's more advanced PC manufacturing technology, and unfettered access to IBM's international resources, including global sales channels and operations teams. The acquisition immediately launched us as a player in developed markets, with one of the world's leading, high-end PC brands, and gave us a presence in every corner of the globe.

The announcement, made on China's national holiday, May Day, filled Lenovo employees with pride. For them, IBM had long been the exemplar of how to do business as a global high-tech company. It was everything we aspired to be. For Liu Chuanzhi, it was a moment of introspection and humility as he looked back on his early days as one of many distribution agents for the computer giant and considered just how far Lenovo had come.

"I remember the first time I took part in a meeting of IBM agents in the 1980s," he recently shared, reminiscing about how far Lenovo had come. "I was wearing an old business suit of my father's and I sat in the back row. Even in my dreams, I never imagined that one day we could buy the IBM PC business. It was unthinkable. Impossible."[4]

There was jubilation in the United States as well. While there was a natural fear of postmerger downsizing, many people at IBM PC had been waiting for something like this to happen. IBM's leaders had long considered IBM PC a peripheral business, and those inside that division who were ambitious felt like poor stepchildren instead of an essential piece of the core business. The Lenovo deal made them feel relevant again; they were a part of something new and groundbreaking. In celebration, IBM sent camera teams to offices in Beijing and Raleigh, North Carolina, to film video greetings between Eastern and Western colleagues. At the call center in Raleigh, employees filmed themselves triumphantly throwing their old IBM badges into the trash.[5]

A Postmerger Period
Rife with Misunderstanding

The excitement was palpable on both sides of the globe. Of course, no one knew exactly how the snake would digest the elephant or just how bad a case of indigestion we were about to face.

The unwelcoming reception that Gina and her Lenovo colleagues faced when they arrived at our offices in Raleigh was just one of many simple misunderstandings that hampered the flow of business in the early days of the merger. Of course, the slights were unintentional on the part of the IBM PC employees. It simply never occurred to them to extend themselves to such a degree. They didn't do it for other out-of-town colleagues, and they had no idea of the kind of logistical challenges that someone from China might face in a brand-new environment. They couldn't put themselves in their Chinese colleagues' shoes because this was the first time something like this had ever been tried. No one in the history of the IT industry had ever been in their situation.

Another trip to Raleigh a few months after the merger demonstrates just how ill equipped to handle the newcomers the people at IBM PC were. When Gina tried to enter the building, the young girl at the reception desk didn't even bother to look up at her. Instead, she asked Gina a few questions, and Gina felt like she was crossing the border once again. She could make out only the words "name tag" and "who are you looking for?" She had no ID, and she knew only that she should ask for "Peter." At that moment, Gina couldn't remember the last name of her direct counterpart in HR at IBM PC.

"Well, that will be difficult," the receptionist said, rolling her eyes. "We have over one hundred Peters here. Which one are you looking for?"

Gina was stumped, and the girl, who was simply doing her job and following the company rules, refused to let her past reception. She wondered why it should be so hard to walk into the offices of a company that Lenovo had just acquired. As she waited in the reception area, feeling humiliated, someone she'd had meetings with in Hong Kong recognized her and helped to sign her in. Only later did she find out that several other Lenovo executives, even YY and Mary Ma, who was our CFO, had received the same treatment.

Everyone at Lenovo China, even those in the highest ranks, felt that they were at a distinct disadvantage. But there was a good reason for it. Our leaders had made the decision to make English the official language of the new corporate entity, even though it put them at a huge disadvantage. Understanding that more global experience was needed to see the merged company through the transition, Chairman Liu took a backseat, and YY effectively stepped aside so that IBM PC veteran executive Steve Ward could take his place as CEO. At the time of the acquisition, Chairman Liu focused instead on the rest of the Legend Group and gave the title of Lenovo chairman to YY.

It was part of our leaders' long-term, strategic thinking. In their wisdom, they understood that, internally and externally, IBM PC employees and customers needed the sense of stability that having one of their own at the helm would create. Gina herself was effectively put on a lower rung; she was no longer in charge of HR now that it was a global business function, but instead was partnering with her new U.S. colleagues, acting as the bridge between Beijing and what were then completely separate departments in the West.

One Lenovo Strategy: Cultivate a Zero Mindset

For longtime Lenovo employees, it was incredibly humbling, but they did what was asked of them. After years of being in the top position in China's market, they swallowed their pride and started all over again, from the bottom.

Past Success Doesn't Count

In order to succeed at Lenovo, you have to have a zero mindset. This means that it doesn't matter whether you were successful in the past. That is the past. You can't assume that the same things that made you successful can be applied to the new environment. When you start a new journey, full of change, you need to look again and acknowledge that you are right back at zero.

When you are a leader, if you feel that you can manage all things already, you have no motivation to learn something new. Because you feel you are already full, you can't put more inside. A zero mindset makes you eager to learn and gives you the opportunity to understand a new environment in depth and see what works best now, instead of simply replicating what was done in past.

—Johnson Jia, Vice President, Lenovo PC Global Operations

Johnson Jia, who today oversees global operations for our PC group, was one of many people at Lenovo who were willing to start over and over again. He and Gina were willing to be humble enough to recognize what they did not know and to set about learning and developing as executives. It's why they've remained and risen to the top. In fact, as hard as the transitions have been, these people thrive on the challenge.

A zero mindset certainly applied to our collective language skills in those first years following the acquisition. While some Lenovo leaders who'd been working with Western suppliers and channel partners had picked up just enough language proficiency over the years to get by, most people at Lenovo, including YY and Gina, found learning English is one of the greatest challenges of their careers. Having studied Japanese as her second language in school, Gina had almost no English vocabulary apart from "hello," "goodbye," and "thank you." So when the decision to make English the official language was first announced, in 2005, her heart sank. She understood the reason why (English is the global language of business), but it was overwhelming.

Switching languages was an extraordinary move for any company that takes over another business. Usually, the home base dictates the culture of a newly merged, global business. Some technology companies have only one headquarters, based in their country of origin, and their local customs tend to dominate the other regional cultures as they expand. Documents are translated into the home language for the top leaders, who are almost entirely of the same nationality and culture, and employees in other countries travel to them, not the other way around. These are businesses with a global reach, but their culture is local, and they view the world through their own regional lens. Lenovo's leaders decided that it should be the other way around. Overnight, we were no longer a Chinese company. This was to be a complete makeover. We were going to become global from the top down, with multiple headquarters and top executives from all corners of the world.

Of course, making the decision was much easier than the execution. Gina, along with leaders like YY and other leaders, hit the books like a good student, taking lessons, diligently memorizing words and phrases, and methodically building up her vocabulary week by week, month by month. She even hired a teacher and set herself vocabulary targets.

But, as she quickly discovered, learning in a classroom or through books did not prepare her to survive the real world of the JFK airport terminal or a New York taxi ride. The work environment was even more challenging. Working in a company that was now four times the size, with multiple divisions and offices around the world, required much more communication through many layers of people.

"When we were local, we could speak in shorthand," explains Johnson. "We understood our environment very well, and people knew one another, so they could make a judgment call quickly. People had the same context in mind. But when overseas colleagues come in, you've got to explain the context."

Different Business Practices
Can Get Lost in Translation

There was no context in those first months after the acquisition. Even a translator couldn't help bridge the gap in understanding, because many of the most basic business concepts were different. IBM PC was managed through comprehensive business processes that had accumulated over more than two decades. These were what the people at IBM PC knew, and, on many levels, the processes worked for a company of IBM's size. But Lenovo was still small and nimble, accustomed to reacting to the local market quickly and thinking on its feet. We paid much less attention to process, learning as we went. So when the two sides got together, these divergent mindsets made it hard to reach consensus on decisions; this led to long meetings and complicated discussions, with end results that didn't turn out as expected. Opportunities were lost, and people were frustrated. Everyone suffered.

Gina was at the heart of some of the most nerve-racking discussions. Once the deal was officially announced, the real negotiations began: salaries, retention benefits, bonus structures, and who was to stay and who was to go. Gina and her small team of HR partners started racking up air miles the moment the ink was dry. These conversations were going to be delicate at best, because in order to make the acquisition work, it was essential that we retain IBM PC's best employees. We needed them to feel confident in the future and, in turn, to make corporate customers believe. But at the same time, IBM PC was in debt. The company was bloated, too many of the people on the payroll were complacent, and the company was losing money to the tune of about $100 million a year. As is the case with most mergers, some painful cuts had to be made.

Within the newly created Lenovo China and Lenovo International business units, we formed project teams to support different functions: sales, finance, purchasing, and so on. Lenovo and IBM PC leaders took ownership of the integration of these teams, which would be split more or less evenly between Eastern and Western employees. Even the board of directors would reflect the balance of East and West. It was to be an integration at all levels, with a multinational management team to rival that of any global computer company.[6]

The Lenovo Way: Put the Needs of the Company First

Our teams needed to make some tough adjustments. Adding to the challenges was the fact that Lenovo employees' pay scale and bonus system were completely different from IBM PC's. Lenovo China's salaries were much lower, but compensation was tied much more aggressively to bonuses, so if our business units were doing well and we were meeting our sales targets, the rewards more than made up for the lower wages. But this meant that if we moved some of our best performers in China to the global business unit, their incomes would drop, because IBM PC's sales had been suffering for years. Some compromises had to be made to deal with some of the differences in the companies' compensation and benefit policies. Thousands of people were going to be affected by the changes. Gina needed to meet with her HR counterparts in New York to get on the same page on some of the most sensitive changes that were about to happen.

But the meeting discussion took place in rapid fire, with Gina's English-speaking colleague Yi Min (who is currently our director of culture integration) struggling to keep up with the translation and getting confused by the corporate jargon.

Gina started to cry. She couldn't imagine how we could even start coming together as one team, one company, if she couldn't understand what was going on. She took 10 minutes, and she and Yi Min went for a walk around the building. Gina felt hopeless and was mortified that her IBM PC counterparts had seen her emotions get the better of her. She was concerned that she was going to let everyone down and wondered how she could do her job if she couldn't understand anything that was being discussed in the meeting. In fact, she almost quit that day.

Slow It Down: Give Everyone in the Room a Chance to Understand

The solution was simple: take a few items off the meeting agenda and slow it down in order to give everyone in the room a chance to process the information. This is a very useful strategy.

People had to be constantly reminded of the need to slow down. Those who are used to one culture, one way of doing things, don't change overnight, and when a concept is foreign to them, it's not enough to translate the words. When the subject of dealing with workers' unions came up, for example, Gina and her team were completely at sea. In China, unions aren't strong political organizations as they are in the West. Instead, they are "workers' councils"—essentially minor government bodies that organize events like movies for employees. They have no significance in employee relations, so Lenovo's

China team was puzzled as to why the topic of unions kept coming up. They understood the literal meaning of the word, but not the implication. It was a complete disconnect.

One Company with Two Systems

Instead of trying to reconcile the differences, most of us worked in our own separate ways, using the processes and habits that we knew from our past. In the first couple of years after the acquisition, it was one company with two systems, and in some ways that was part of the plan. YY had always called the deal a "marriage of equals." His willingness to relinquish his CEO position; move our company headquarters to the U.S.; make English the official language; and, in effect, come to IBM PC instead of the other way around were all demonstrations of his commitment to this approach.

Our leaders were taking the long view. Liu Chuanzhi and YY both knew how nervous the world was about a Chinese company taking over IBM's PC division. We'd seen the dire predictions in the media that there was no way we could absorb such a behemoth of a company, that we had aimed too high, and that we would surely fail. It wasn't just that we were a relatively small local company taking over an iconic American multinational; we were *Chinese*. China was perceived as the world's factory, making cheap, shoddy, low-tech consumer goods and unfamiliar with the ways of Western-style commerce. Many people, both inside and outside of China, could not imagine that we would ever become a sophisticated global IT company.

The bias against us came out in many forms, even involving national security. There was media chatter in the U.S. at the time of the acquisition that Chinese influence on Lenovo could lead to spyware in its PCs. And the resistance to Chinese ownership wasn't limited to the United States. At the former IBM PC office in Japan, the newly integrated employees rebelled. The engineers, in particular, refused to take any design direction from Beijing, clinging to the old design of the ThinkPad notebooks, which were inspired by the Japanese "lunchbox" and had not changed much in more than a decade.[7]

So the immediate goal was to maintain stability by creating a sense that nothing had really changed. IBM PC was still IBM. Lenovo just happened to be the owner, but things would still be run exactly the way they had been run for the past three decades. As part of the initial deal, Lenovo even kept the IBM logo on the ThinkPad computers.

Of course it couldn't go on this way. If our people were to feel pride in who we were, we needed to grow and evolve. We were like a patient after an operation who needs to stay still while vital signs are being closely monitored. The deal hadn't fallen apart, but Lenovo had lost the sense of cohesion that had brought it to the number one spot in China. We were losing some great people, and our ThinkPad division was bleeding red ink. Many in the media were speculating that "Chinese ineptitude" would surely sink a great global brand name. It was time for some major changes, even if that meant losing more people.

Someone once described the situation as "nearly complete organ rejection."[8] No one could imagine how we could merge two companies with such divergent business models across 12 time zones, especially in the highly competitive IT environment, where, every month, someone comes out with a new technology that can make a bestseller obsolete. The odds seemed stacked against us. Michael Dell, chairman of Dell, publicly pronounced us dead on arrival. "It won't work," he said.[9]

Remember Just How Important Communication Is

Despite these negative perceptions, there were many early signs that East and West could eventually become a workable blend. Throughout the company, there were ongoing efforts to smooth out some of the kinks in the early stages of the integration process—on both sides of the cultural divide. Most of this was happening naturally, on an individual basis, as professional relationships were forming across borders and evolving into friendships. Other people were more deliberate in their approach.

Crystal Arrington, our present-day corporate ombudsman at Lenovo, was one of a small group of IBM executives who had the empathy and the sensitivity to break through the communication barrier early on. She had a way with people that was instinctive and cut across the cultural divide, making her an ideal cultural bridge.

Crystal recalls being on a conference call between Gina and her HR counterpart in the United States, a former IBM employee who was based in New York. Crystal sensed a communication gap and listened carefully as Gina and her colleague were discussing the relocation plan for executives. There were no international assignment rules at the time. We were just defining the process as we went along, and Gina's counterpart was thinking on his feet as he was speaking with Gina, assuming that it was a brainstorming session where they could come up with solutions by thinking out loud. Finally, at the end of the conversation, he summed up what he thought was the content of the conversation, defining what he believed should be the terms of any executive relocation.

"Okay, great. So now I guess we have a plan, and that's how we'll proceed," he said. Gina remained silent on the other end of the phone. He assumed that her silence meant that she had no objections, but Crystal wasn't so sure.

A couple of weeks later, Crystal traveled to Beijing to meet with the executives she would be helping to relocate, and with Gina. At that point, nothing that had been discussed on the phone had been implemented. Crystal could sense that Gina had felt bulldozed. She entered the Lenovo headquarters and took the elevator up to the third floor. When the doors opened, there was Gina, a woman Crystal barely knew, except through a handful of meetings and conference calls. But Gina recognized her immediately and gave her a big hug.

At that point, Gina still didn't speak the language, so a member of her staff joined them in Gina's office to translate. After exchanging a few pleasantries, Crystal said, "Gina, I noticed that you didn't say anything in the meeting. How do you really feel?"

When the assistant finished translating the question, Gina smiled, happy for the chance to be understood. She explained to Crystal that she had been silent on the call because she did not agree, but she did not want to be disrespectful to her colleague, adding that she felt surprised and frustrated that he was moving forward on his end, pushing his plan without her explicit agreement. She'd been struggling to find a nice way to tell him that she had a different opinion.

Crystal explained that in the West, people are very direct and open in how they communicate, so it is assumed that if nothing is said and there are no objections, everyone is on the same page. Then she taught Gina a sentence that she could use in future meetings as a face-saving way of letting people know that she wasn't on board: "I am not comfortable." Gina has used that phrase many times since.

Once Gina understood the different working styles, she became more vocal with her colleague, who eventually learned to take her pauses in conversation as cues to ask her directly for her input. This went a long way toward speeding up the decision-making process and enabling them to implement their plans more efficiently.

Don't Discount the Small Stuff: Even a Gesture Can Boost Morale

Steve Crutchfield, our director of site operations in Raleigh, was another IBM veteran who was making a concerted effort to make his new Eastern colleagues feel comfortable, welcomed, and respected. When the acquisition happened, he read a book, *Chinese Business Etiquette* by Scott Seligman, and circulated it around the office[10] to make sure that everyone was prepared for any differences in style.

Hearing about the failure to meet and greet our Eastern executives properly during their earlier trips, he also put in place protocols for overseas visitors. Noticing that his Eastern counterparts seemed anxious to have plenty of bottled water for meetings, he even made sure to stock plenty of bottled water at our Raleigh offices, as well as electric water kettles for the desktops of visiting executives from Lenovo China, who preferred to drink hot water and tea.

Get Personal: Speaking from the Heart Cuts across Cultures

Gina also learned to play the role of cultural bridge, calming the frayed nerves of her IBM PC counterparts. In those early meetings, she was quick to let them know that she could relate to their concerns. She told them the story of her first experience with layoffs, when Legend had had an internal merger of sales departments that had cost dozens of jobs. She frequently shared the story of how devastated and resentful she felt when she saw her colleagues, some of whom were her closest friends, leave the company after many years, and how deeply she related to everyone's concerns.

Late in 2005, morale was low in the Raleigh office, where the bulk of IBM PC's operations were based. "People were jittery," recalls Peter Hortensius. On a brief visit, he asked Gina to talk to the staff, to let them know that those on the Lenovo China team were colleagues, working for their best interests.

Gina was nervous. Although her English language skills had improved considerably, she was extremely uncomfortable speaking in front of a large group of people, particularly in another language. More than a thousand employees gathered in the company cafeteria, the only space big enough to accommodate that many people at the time. For most of them, Gina was the first face they'd seen from their new owners in China, so she knew that she was being judged. But she put herself in their shoes, somehow finding just the right words to put their minds at ease. Her warmth and humanity came through.

Even with her broken English, Peter still remembers the impact she made. It came through loud and clear that this wasn't just a job for her; it was family. Hearing that message, sensing her compassion, and being able to associate a kind face with what until then had been anonymous investors all the way over in Beijing, made all the difference.

Lenovo Strategy Takeaways

- Play the long game—think in terms of years, not short-term gains.

- Recognize the gap between where you are and what you intend to become.

- Tension is positive; it challenges your people to think a whole new way.

- Leverage the employees who are ready, willing, and able to change.

- Expect fallout and discomfort from a merger, then deal with it.

- Understand that clear communication goes beyond language.

CHAPTER 4

Leading
through Chaos

Lenovo Principle 3: Identify What's Broken,
Then Use Every Internal and External Resource
to Fix It.

t didn't take long for Peter Hortensius, who by now had become one of our unofficial cross-cultural ambassadors, to figure out that developing a personal relationship with each of his
team members in China would go a long way toward fostering
trust. In some cases, it happened naturally. For example, Peter
and George He, now SVP of Ecosystem and Cloud Services,
clicked from the moment they met because they already had a
common language and frame of reference.

"We were both engineers, so we understood each other
pretty well," Peter recalls. "When you think the way we do, there
are only a few ways to solve a problem, and we both wanted
the same thing—to create great products that could enhance
the lives of ordinary customers."

Of course, Peter wasn't completely new to China, and George, who had been among the first to be sent to Hong Kong to start product development and manufacturing, had had plenty of contact with Westerners over the years. By the time George and Peter met, George's English was close to fluent, he was a huge fan of Peter's work in developing the Think product line, and the two men genuinely liked each other. He became the perfect gateway for Peter as he got to know his peers in China. Peter, for his part, recognized that Lenovo China's strengths were the perfect complement to those of IBM PC. His Eastern colleagues knew how to make high-quality, inexpensive products and sell high volumes into one of the most challenging consumer markets in the world. Combining the two companies' respective strengths could lead to something great: a middle way that would reach millions more consumers around the globe.

It helped that Peter was willing to get on a plane and travel to China. He'd been there a few times before the acquisition for meetings with his IBM China colleagues and also with suppliers and manufacturers. But he quickly realized that his understanding of Eastern culture didn't go deep enough.

"Most of the teams we'd been dealing with in China and Japan were already Westernized. They had to be, in order to survive in a Western company. And when you are dealing with suppliers, you are their customers, and they are trying to sell you something, so of course they are going to see things your way."

Peter had never fully appreciated the differences in culture and mindset, or the degree to which these differences drove business decisions. Just when he thought something had been understood and agreed upon, he found that it wasn't. The Eastern and Western teams couldn't draw upon obvious analogies or use expressions and terms that could immediately clarify or deepen their message.

"It was difficult for both sides, not because of animosity, but because of the constant need to read between the lines and figure out, 'What did they really mean?'"

Even with the best translators, either there was no comprehension, or, even worse, an expression would be taken literally, which meant that the Chinese team would walk away thinking completely the wrong thing.

"There was a significant lack of appreciation on my part as to just how big the cultural difference was going to be in this. My IBM colleagues and I thought that we'd got it, but we hadn't. We thought we were more global than we were. But the Lenovo team *knew* that they weren't global. They already understood just how much they had to learn. It took the IBM team a little while longer to figure that out."

> Take stock. When you are undergoing a major change, it's essential that you step back and take a good, hard look, even when the view is uncomfortable.

We had to be willing to drill down deep, do a full and painful diagnosis of what was really going on at all levels of the company, and acknowledge exactly where we were failing. Sometimes that requires bringing in people from outside, who can be objective and provide a fresh perspective on a problem and a new take on what the solution might be.

We could have said that just holding steady was enough and continued with the status quo. From a business perspective, we'd already achieved a degree of stability, not to mention considerable cost savings. Immediately following the acquisition, Mary Ma and her team had taken a scalpel to IBM PC's bloated books. Their target: to trim roughly $150 million within 18 months. The numbers were like nothing they'd ever seen— 1 percent in savings equaled $100 million, or Lenovo's average annual profit at the time. But they succeeded, exceeding their target within eight months by bringing down procurement and manufacturing costs and improving the company's travel policy to reduce waste and abuses in travel expenses. So Lenovo was quick to find and exploit every opportunity to improve IBM PC's financial and operational efficiency.[1]

Within a year of the acquisition, we'd also launched operations and introduced our brand in more than 65 countries, with few glitches in deliveries or support. We had managed to hold on to most of our customers, we had retained 98 percent of our employees, and we'd gained global market share, putting us at number three in the world behind HP and Dell.[2]

Given the high failure rate of mergers in the IT industry, our performance was actually pretty good, although it wasn't good enough. We had to take more drastic action, beginning with our people and the way our teams interacted. The relationships that were being built by individuals like Crystal, Gina, Peter, and George were certainly having a ripple effect, but we needed to find ways to duplicate these efforts on a more companywide level. Individual efforts can fall short. The kind of deep, sweeping changes that were needed to facilitate full integration required more radical steps that would change people's behavior from the top down. We had to completely turn the tide.

Changing of the Guard

The process began with another leadership change. By the end of December 2005, IBMer Steve Ward, our transitional CEO and president, who had come with the acquisition of the PC division, had moved on. This time we didn't choose an insider to replace him. For now, YY would have to continue to take something of a backseat in the less active role of chairman. Instead, we brought in Bill Amelio.

To call Bill a brilliant IT executive would be an understatement. Formerly senior vice president of Dell, Lenovo's biggest competitor, he'd most recently served as president of Asia-Pacific and Japan for Dell. For many years now, YY had observed just how aggressive and smart Dell's growth strategy in Asia had been. Both Dell and Lenovo were similar in that they were both original equipment manufacturers (OEMs) that produced affordable PCs that they marketed and sold aggressively. Lenovo's sales team had learned a great deal over the years by observing their rival's direct sales strategy. IBM had none of this experience. So bringing in a top executive from Dell was the kind of shot in the arm needed to drive the operational excellence that Lenovo needed.

"With our integration of IBM's PC division on track and our organizational integration complete, we are accelerating our planning for our next phase of growth," YY announced at the time. "Bill Amelio's combined experience—in our industry, in emerging and mature markets, in senior operational roles, and with IBM—gives him the perfect profile to lead Lenovo from the important stability we have achieved in the first phase of our integration to the profitable growth and efficiency improvement to which we are committed in our next phase."

Bill was collaborative in his own way, results-driven, and a stickler for numbers and details. Immediately after the acquisition, we had to work fast to stem losses and bring in new sources of revenue, and Bill had the ability to drill down into the books and do just that. It was a style that was different from anything we'd ever known, and it was a fresh perspective that we needed at the time.

When he arrived at Lenovo, Bill wasted no time putting together his dream team. We hired from everywhere: Dell, McKinsey Consulting, Microsoft, Acer, HP. . . . Potentially, this unique situation was an enormous competitive advantage. It spurred us to even more globalization. In order to attract top talent, we had to allow our executives to be based in more locations around the world and to work remotely. Doing so put us in a position to leverage multiple strengths and points of view. We could become globally and culturally diverse in the truest sense, something that very few other multinationals have achieved. But, if anything, it was making us even more fragmented. Pieces of the mosaic were scattered all over the place.

Bridging the East/West Divide

There were deep clashes among some of the Western leaders, as well as between the Western leaders and Lenovo's China team members, who weren't used to the more aggressive approach of many of the former Dell employees' management style. The Western leaders, meanwhile, were not accustomed to the secretive, noncommunicative approach that was more typical of the Eastern workplace culture.

A case in point was Chen Xudong, currently SVP of China and Asia Pacific–Emerging Markets, who was one of our stars in sales. Working under the newly appointed Asia-Pacific team out of Singapore nearly drove him to leave Lenovo.

We had just undergone another major restructuring. The management changes a year earlier had led to a much tighter integration of key business functions such as product development, supply chain management, planning, and control, as well as sales and marketing. To support these changes, we implemented a new, companywide IT system that allowed us to ship to more than 100 countries. This streamlining also led to some drastic downsizing in March 2006, when we laid off more than 1,000 people out of an employee population of 21,400, spread evenly across all regions.[3] That year, we also relocated our U.S. corporate headquarters from Purchase, New York, to Raleigh, North Carolina.

Our sales teams were hit especially hard as we split our geographical regions into four of what we call the "Geos": China, Asia-Pacific, the Americas, and EMEA (Europe, the Middle East, and Africa). There were a lot of internal adjustments to be made, and not just because of the reorganization. The entire Asia-Pacific operation had just been moved from Sydney to Singapore, and not everyone was pleased with the relocation.

Xudong was put in charge of sales and distribution for the Asia-Pacific region. His first challenge was dealing with the expectation of multiple reports and continuous number crunching.

"We were being hammered to deliver numbers—monthly, weekly, daily," recalls Xudong. "It was very short-term-driven, and there was a lot of pressure."

Xudong spent most of his time in "review meetings" with spreadsheets and PowerPoints. Having spent his entire career at Lenovo China, which was more focused on trying to figure out and execute a strategy that was appropriate for the situation on the ground, this data-driven approach wasn't what he was accustomed to. Typically, Xudong would be in 15 or 20 meetings a week, including 6 meetings with each of the region's sales leaders, more meetings just to prepare for meetings with his boss at the time, and the actual review meeting. It was self-defeating, because all that focus on short-term gains forced him to divert his attention from implementing the very sales strategy that would help him get those numbers.

"We were under that pressure because of a lack of trust," Xudong explained to us later. "Because the people on the top management team didn't trust those at the execution level, they wanted to review every detail to the point where we didn't have time to do our actual jobs."

His and Gina's experiences were almost parallel. Around the same time, Gina was also relocated to Singapore, where she oversaw HR for the Asia-Pacific group. Her English, though much improved, still wasn't fluent, and the leadership team was often impatient with her in meetings, frequently talking over her or dismissing what she had to say. Because they underestimated her, she had less to do, and she felt completely sidelined. Xudong and Gina, who had become close friends through their joint expatriate experiences, often got together for barbecues on weekends or dinners after work to compare notes. It was the opposite problem from the one that Xudong had, but it boiled down to the same thing: lack of trust.

Both Xudong and Gina had opportunities to go back to China, but they decided to stay for the same reason:

"I really wanted to open my eyes and see a different world," Xudong explained. "And if I moved back, in some way I would feel like a failure. I just didn't want to give up."

Many others did give up. We lost several good people from both East and West during this transitional period. Some of them couldn't handle the late night phone calls overseas. Others with young families weren't comfortable with all the travel. A handful of our colleagues from China felt that their language skills would never measure up to the demands of their new role and chose to step down, putting the best interests of Lenovo before their own. The rest simply found the new environment, with its pervading sense of distrust, too toxic.

Bring in a Change Agent

Stepping into this situation was another Dell veteran, Yolanda Lee Conyers. When she was first hired in January 2007, there was plenty of cynicism about the arrival of yet another former Dell employee. It was generally assumed that Yolanda was another member of Bill's FOBs (all the Dell hires were referred as "Friends of Bill"). Most people believed that Yolanda had been hired to pad out his forces of like-minded IT executives. Even Gina said so, and questioned why Yolanda was being hired. But that was before Yolanda's new colleagues realized that she was an altogether different breed of executive, one whose experience, insights, and presence would go far in easing tensions and one of the Westerners who would lead the creation of a brand new culture that combined the best of East and West.

Yolanda had been with Dell since 1991—the first African American female hired as a software engineer in the company. A fiercely loyal employee who'd spent her career working long hours, Yolanda had risen through the ranks from junior and middle management positions in product development, sales, customer service, and human resources and procurement in the global supply chain, earning her an executive title. Her experience and knowledge cut across multiple business functions.

Most important, however, was her deep understanding of and passion for the need to create a workplace that was inclusive, one in which all points of view, backgrounds, and experiences were valued and blended into the corporate culture. She was known for successfully leading globally diverse teams, leveraging her program and operational management skills to drive for results with diverse teams. And she had received internal and external recognition for her work in high-tech industries during her tenure at Texas Instruments and at Dell.

Yolanda was ready for this change. Serious health problems following the birth of her second son in 2005 and six months of doctor-ordered bed rest during her pregnancy had forced her to slow down and take some time away from the office. This distance from Dell gave her a new perspective on her work/life balance, prompting her to resign with no idea of what she would do next. Yolanda needed a change, and she needed the time and space to think about what she really wanted from her career. If she was going to jump back into the IT industry again, it had to be in a role that she was truly passionate about, something that would make it worth the time she would be spending away from her family. So when the chance to establish the first diversity office at Lenovo was presented to her, she jumped at it.

Yolanda made two trips to Raleigh for interviews. In the first, she met with Bill, an executive she remembered well from her days at Dell. She'd always admired his global leadership skills, finding him to be smart and an excellent executor who had the ability to take people with him. In the interview, he was candid about the challenges he was facing and how different the environment was at Lenovo.

"We are making history at Lenovo," he told her. Yolanda's second trip included an interview with YY. She was especially nervous about speaking with Lenovo's chairman, although that did not diminish her excitement that the chairman of any company would be this interested and engaged in an interview process. It was a strong sign that Lenovo was serious about integrating diversity into its culture.

Yolanda had learned early in her career to ask for help when she needed it, and she always leveraged the best resources to learn. To prepare for this interview, she reached out to an executive coach for CEOs and senior vice presidents who had years of global experience, especially in China. She has never forgotten the advice he gave her: "Be humble with YY and tell him up front that you understand cultural diversity primarily from an American's perspective. Let him know that, if you take the position, you would need to learn from him."

He told her that in order to become a respected leader as the head of cultural integration and not just an American diversity leader with a global title, she needed to show an openness to learning about Chinese culture, as well as the other cultures represented by the Lenovo employee population.

The interview went so well that during the interview, YY told her, "Yolanda, you would be a great fit for Lenovo. I am going to tell my team that the job is yours if you want it."

She had long been frustrated with the limits of diversity as it was typically practiced in most U.S. organizations, focusing more on quotas than on fostering an inclusive environment that fosters diversity. So when the Lenovo offer came, she didn't hesitate to accept it. This was her chance to make a difference and provide the leadership needed to work with Lenovo's unique and challenging global diversity in a way that could have real meaning and value in our workplace.

As always, YY was willing to try something new. He stayed committed to his vision of successful cultural integration by leveraging a more Western approach and doing whatever was necessary to ensure that all voices could be heard. Both he and Liu Chuanzhi recognized that the success of the acquisition depended on how well Lenovo's people communicated and worked together, and they had already spent many hours drilling down into ways that this could happen. So when YY met Yolanda, the decision was easy. Yolanda was named chief diversity officer, reporting to the senior vice president of

> Be open to an outside perspective. Sometimes that requires bringing in people from outside, who can be objective, have a fresh take on an ongoing problem, and have some new insights into what the solution might be.

human resources. It was the first time anyone in any industry had held that title in a Chinese company. Once again, Lenovo was making history.

Creating a Corporate United Nations

Of course, Yolanda hadn't been on the job long before she realized that this would not be like any other global leadership role she'd held in the past, but she plunged headlong into what would become the greatest challenge of her career thus far.

On January 17, 2007, Yolanda's first day on the job, a critical meeting commissioned by Bill Amelio was taking place, and she'd flown into Beijing for it. She joined members of our senior leadership team, along with consultants from McKinsey and Pathpoint Consulting, who were presenting the results of a major culture audit. When Yolanda walked in the room she was amazed by the diversity—it looked like the General Assembly of the United Nations. Yolanda had never seen so much cultural and national diversity at this high level, all gathered together in one place.

The meeting was overwhelming and exhilarating at the same time. The atmosphere in the room was charged as everyone in the room listened intently to the results of the audit. The consultant delivering the data was fluent in Chinese, and he shifted back and forth between English and Mandarin to ensure that everyone in the room understood the content. It was at that moment that Yolanda realized that one of the major diversity issues affecting Lenovo was the vast difference in languages and the basic ability to communicate. This was not going to be easy.

Highlight the Strengths and Identify the Weaknesses

After the meeting, Yolanda spent time with the consultants from McKinsey, as well as Pathpoint, to further distill and understand the results of the audit before coming up with some action plans.

The report was part of an effort that had been launched just before Yolanda joined, and it was our first full physical assessment since the acquisition. Over the course of four weeks at the end of 2006, many interviews had been conducted across 25 countries, with input from all levels of the company. On the plus side, the report found that despite the problems, employees believed in the future, were willing to commit, and had a great sense of pride in our heritage. But there were some major challenges—stumbling blocks that we had recognized instinctively over the year and a half since the acquisition—laid out in the stark bullets of a PowerPoint:

- Trust. There was a high degree of skepticism concerning colleagues' intentions and capabilities.

- Accountability. There was a lack of comfort with the target-setting process, amount of tolerance for missing targets, and acceptance of excuses.

- Direction. Employees were not sure whether the company had a clear strategy and vision and were unsure about how to make decisions and trade-offs.

- Execution. People felt that the company was moving slowly and was wasting tremendous amounts of time and energy.

- Capability. The company lacked the skills and capabilities of a global company and was not investing in the systems it needed to attract talent and develop its people.

- Innovation. Some employees did not feel encouraged to develop and implement new ideas or share new concepts across the company.

What the audit found was that lack of trust was the most significant issue—the root cause of much of the tension. Until that was repaired, none of the other global issues could be addressed. People could not come together on anything. Some of the direct quotes from the employees interviewed were, "Everyone feels like they are being taken over," "This is not a performance culture, it is an excuse culture," and "We are all very anxious and want to make this work; however, we sometimes feel we are alone . . . and very unclear about our direction." There was distrust between the local and regional offices, or what we call our Geos, and the global team. There was anger and frustration over the fact that it felt like Lenovo was multiple companies, each following its own rules rather than working together as one unified whole.

These feelings were universal. Colleagues in many Lenovo offices felt isolated, as if they were working in their own bubble, disconnected even from those who were working in the next cubicle. Jeanne Bauer, our current HR business partner of the PC Product Group based in Raleigh, was shocked by how siloed we were when she first joined Lenovo in June 2007.

"It was all so decentralized in HR. Whether it was compensation, benefits, or other programs, everyone was following their own process—what they knew from their previous employer," Jeanne recalls. Incentive programs and even job titles were not consistent. "The IBMers were sticking with what they knew, the Dell people were using what they'd learned at Dell, and the local offices were making it up as they went along. And they all insisted on hanging on to their own processes. It was *chaos*!"

It seemed to take forever to make a decision and execute. People were approaching their work from so many conflicting angles that it created a logjam. As an outsider coming in with a fresh perspective, Jeanne could see what was happening, and she recognized the challenges that we faced working together. Jeanne had joined from NCR, an IT multinational that was then based in the Midwest and was much more homogenous, in 2007. She'd never experienced an environment as diverse as the one she found at Lenovo, which, after multiple hires from different corporations and countries, had become a frayed patchwork that was barely hanging together. "The mentality was, 'I was hired to do a job: they wanted me for my experience, and this is what I bring.' You could see that there was going to be a culture clash if somebody didn't step in soon."

> The causes of culture clashes are more complex than simply language barriers and national differences.

Interview People Face to Face

Now that she fully understood the diagnosis, Yolanda spent the next two months meeting with the key players face to face. She held meetings with her HR colleagues, led roundtables with employees and leaders of Lenovo's various business groups, and conducted one-on-one meetings with the CEO and his direct reports, so that she could get even more clarity concerning the audit results. In particular, she was trying to understand exactly what was driving this profound lack of trust. She wanted to go deeper in order to fully grasp what the culture and diversity tensions were.

Armed with that knowledge, she began to work closely with our top leadership team to come up with a concrete action plan. In her meetings, Yolanda was struck by how seriously our leaders were taking the problems. This went all the way to the top: YY, our chairman at the time; Bill, our CEO and president; and all the senior vice presidents. She saw the vulnerability in everyone and sensed the urgency to get the situation fixed.

Doing this was going to be tough. It takes incredible leadership to bring in people from the outside to objectively take stock and hear all sides, because the leaders doing so have to be willing to concede that they may be part of the problem. But what was unique about Lenovo at that time was that so many of the people in the top leadership spots were brand-new in their positions. Bill, for example, had never been a CEO before. Several executive vice presidents, both Eastern and Western, were in those positions for the first time, having made the leap from vice president overnight. So there was an acknowledgment from the top down that we were all just feeling our way, and in some ways that made our leaders more open to new approaches and new ways of thinking.

So, as challenging as the situation was, it was also encouraging to see how our top executives were receiving ideas that were being presented by outsiders and newcomers like

Yolanda. Recognizing that diversity and culture clashes started at the top, the CEO, Bill, and her boss gave Yolanda an open invitation to attend all his executive committee meetings. The diversity executive in a corporation often doesn't get a seat at the CEO's table. In this case, however, the top leaders held a spot on the agenda where she could present progress on the culture work, signifying that this wasn't just about compliance with government regulations but a true commitment to diversity and change at the most senior level. It left her in no doubt that this company was serious about diversity.

Corporate Cultures Can Be as Distinct as National Cultures

Yolanda wasted no time; she summarized all her interviews and shared her findings and analysis in a face-to-face meeting with Bill and other senior leaders. What she found was that Lenovo's biggest challenge revolved around national culture differences, particularly those between East and West. Exacerbating these national divides were deep divides in company culture. Both the acquisition and Bill's most recent hires had brought in people from a wide variety of corporate backgrounds. Layered onto that were local and regional diversity challenges, which varied but were not as serious. Because the interviewees had spent all their time providing examples and expressing their frustrations with national and company culture issues, Yolanda recommended a strong focus and investment to address those top two challenges. She stressed that failure to tackle these issues would be the biggest barrier to our future success, as trust is the foundation on which we build as we work with our customers and with one another.

Yolanda then talked about the "three rivers," referring to the factions of our colleagues with histories at IBM, Lenovo, and Dell. We had three main tributaries flowing into the same large body of water, but they weren't flowing together. Each group blamed the others as the source of the problems. Where some people saw fast-moving rapids that were destroying everything in their way, others saw a lazy river that was overflowing its banks.

Specifically, while the Dell hires were commended for their speed, sense of urgency, and drive for data and results, they were also labeled "aggressive and arrogant." They were perceived as valuing speed and results more than people. The IBMers, meanwhile, were appreciated for their innovation and loyalty but were perceived as valuing loyalty over performance. Put more harshly, some were considered "slow-moving and entitled." The Chinese employees at Lenovo were regarded as performance-driven and accountable, yet they were also perceived as "unyielding and unwilling to communicate" and lacking in capability as global leaders.

There was another, fourth tributary that consisted of leaders from other companies. They were perceived as having new ideas and great perspectives. But because they were overpowered by the other three groups, these individuals didn't have much of a voice.

All of this resulted in finger-pointing and tension every time people got together in a room. We needed to stop stereotyping each other, assuming negative intentions, and to start trusting, for the sake of the future of the entire business.

It was clear that we needed a single culture—one that would unite all the rivers. That culture did not exist yet, so everyone was operating from what he or she knew or had experienced in previous companies. It meant that ours was still a culture under construction.

Identify the Positives and Build from There

We had most of the the basic elements of a diverse work culture. Aside from having rich cross-cultural diversity, we also had a large number of women in the organization, though we could have benefited from having more women at the executive level. So, after a few months in the job, we established a women's iniative called Women in Lenovo Leadership. This initiave was designed to promote further development and advancement of women in Lenovo. There was strong support from the top to improve, and with some focus, the number of women in executive-level positions increased significantly.

But when we began our diversity work, the different groups weren't blending together in a cohesive fashion.The tension inspired an urgent need to change, and we became focused on overcoming the obstacles that lay before us and finding solutions that could work for everyone. Diversity pushes people out of their comfort zones and shakes them out of their set patterns of thinking, which can only lead to greater growth.

We had a chance to make corporate history by raising the bar for what was conventionally understood as workplace diversity. Lenovo was already challenging Yolanda's own preconceptions about the term. She had a much more narrowly defined concept of diversity, one that had come out of the unique history and set of circumstances in the United States. But what most organizations in the West and elsewhere fail to grasp is that diversity is about much more than just demographics and equal opportunity—it's actually *good* for business. Many senior HR leaders or diversity practitioners are asked to develop a business case for diversity. Top managers invariably decline to spend money on anything bold and comprehensive because they don't fully grasp the idea that in an increasingly global economy, the greater the diversity of cultures, experiences, and thinking, the better it is for the bottom line. But Yolanda didn't need to make the business case to our senior leaders. They were already sold on its principles.

As Yolanda began to spend more time with her Chinese colleagues, she was impressed by their thoughtful, innovative approach to the integration process, even if they didn't know the lingo of diversity work and their global experience was limited. Instinctively, our Chinese colleagues understood the need for diversity and inclusiveness, despite the fact that the term *diversity* did not even exist in HR practice in China. They also realized that there was room to grow, and they wanted better collaboration with their Western counterparts. As Yolanda started meeting with more of her Chinese colleagues, she discovered that many of them were pioneers in HR in China, with HR degrees from top universities, and that some of them had furthered their education at top universities in the United States. Their insights on how to bridge the China and global businesses were invaluable.

One colleague in particular, Yi Min, a Mongolian Chinese woman who had worked for a global company before joining Lenovo, was quick to embrace Yolanda and her diversity goals.

Yi Min, who had also been Gina's rock during the early transition period after the IBM PC acquisition, became a dear friend, coaching Yolanda on how to navigate the complexities of Chinese culture and offering advice and support in those first few months of culture work.

Motives Can Be Misunderstood

But not everyone immediately came on board with what Yolanda was trying to do. As she learned later from her conversations with both Gina and Yi Min, she was charging ahead before she had taken the time to build relationships and do the kind of trust work that she was advocating for the senior leadership. Overtaken by a sense of urgency, she was rushing toward finding solutions before taking the time to really understand Lenovo's culture and heritage. She wanted results. But she tried to do too much, too soon, and it backfired.

Until they got to know her, many of her colleagues were convinced that she was just another "aggressive American." They didn't fully understand her role. Some of them even believed that she was there just to be a "PR face" for Lenovo's cultural integration efforts. That was why, within a couple of months on the job, Yolanda got a bad review from a few of her Chinese colleagues.

> Acknowledge that you may be part of the problem. Even if you have been brought in to be part of the solution, no one is immune to miscommunications and culture clashes.

One HR team member in particular was more vocal in her complaints. Prior to one of her Beijing trips, Yolanda sent her a note, asking her to schedule a meeting.

"It was very direct," that fomer colleague recalls. "I thought, 'I am busy taking care of the whole of China's HR infrastructure. The entire team reports to me. I am your equal, not your secretary.'"

She was upset that Yolanda didn't ask her opinion about whom she should meet or share details on what the meeting was to be about. She held a fairly senior position and mistook Yolanda's down-to-business style for being bossy. So when the senior vice president of global HR asked her what she thought of Yolanda, she said simply, "I don't like her."

Afterward, over dinner in Hong Kong, Gina gently advised Yolanda of some cultural protocols that would help her smooth her relationships with the China team. It was an extensive list of pointers:

- When you set up a meeting with a Chinese person and then cancel, that shows disrespect. You must keep your commitment. Yolanda had some scheduling issues when she first went to Beijing. There were so many people she needed to meet during that visit that she decided to divide the list and have a senior manager on her team take some of the other meetings.

- When you invite a Chinese executive for a one-on-one meeting, you must be very clear about the purpose of the meeting. And Chinese executives like the email to be directed at them only, not part of a group email, which appears disrespectful. Yolanda's administrative staff, following her direction, sent a group invitation to the executives and their assistants requesting a meeting to discuss diversity and culture integration—a less personal approach that may have offended some people.

- Using the word *disagree* comes across as too strong to the Chinese, and is also considered disrespectful. In general, when you don't agree with someone, the matter must be handled with the utmost sensitivity. The Chinese call this "saving face." Instead of being direct and candid, Yolanda was advised to mix praise with gentle suggestions for improvement. In one of her early conversations, Yolanda had been very tough with her colleague, which was taken to be disrespectful.

- When a relationship has yet to be built, and you make cultural missteps like those just listed, it becomes hard for the Chinese to trust you. Yolanda's colleagues didn't know her, and she didn't know them, so they weren't comfortable. Building trust would require time, patience, and a willingness to listen and to share experiences. Yolanda had to start painstakingly building individual relationships, or what the Chinese call *guanxi* personalized networks that are the foundation of Chinese society.

- When interacting with Chinese colleagues, especially those who are struggling with their English skills, repeat back what they say to show that you understand their point of view. This shows that you are listening.

- Even dress can be misinterpreted as a sign of disrespect. Gina advised Yolanda to wear a jacket to work every day, except for Friday, which was business casual. She was also urged to learn a few key words in Mandarin to show respect for her Chinese colleagues and their culture. A little extra effort would go far.

If Yolanda could make this work, it would help her build trust with her Chinese colleagues. This, in turn, would allow her to have deeper conversations, so that she could better understand the challenges in the East and identify the strategies that could bridge these cultural gaps.

She adapted to some of the feedback and began to make progress. Even the colleague who had complained about her when she first joined Lenovo was impressed by the effort that Yolanda was now making to learn her culture and quickly became her ally. The two women taught each other, and Yolanda's Chinese colleague learned another, more Western way of resolving conflict.

"In Chinese culture, if a child has a problem with a sibling, he goes to his parent. But we are brothers and sisters, so we need to learn how to work it out among ourselves," she later told Yolanda.

Transforming a Culture Is Never a Rush Job

However, far-reaching change wasn't going to happen overnight. The hard work of adjusting mindsets and behavior is an ongoing process that can require a huge investment of time, and our journey of transformation was just beginning. That tough feedback helped Yolanda realize this. Simply parachuting in for two weeks at a time was not enough to develop the kind of *guanxi* she would need in order to truly blend with her new colleagues. So Yolanda made the decision to move to Beijing for three months, without her husband and her two young sons, who would be able to visit only during the summer school break.

She was determined to prove that Eastern and Western colleagues could understand and trust each other, but doing that would require some extended face time. There's a famous saying in Chinese, *san ren xing bi you wo shi*: "When three people walk together, one can be my teacher." That was Yolanda's goal, but it would take patience. This was a process that could not be rushed.

Lenovo Strategy Takeaways

- Cultivate *guanxi*. Strong relationships are the passport to achieving your business goals.

- A lack of trust stymies decision making and frustrates your best people.

- Leverage a fresh perspective. Outsiders can often see more clearly than insiders can.

- Recognize the strengths but identify the weaknesses and then take action to correct them.

- Don't assume that everyone understands your intentions. State them clearly from the outset.

- Sweat the small stuff. When you are doing business in a new culture, study the protocols, as even a seemingly minor misstep can cause a huge offense.

- Cultural integration is never a rush job. It is not a sprint, but rather a journey.

CHAPTER 5

Global World,
Global Thinking

Lenovo Principle 4: Walk the talk. You can't expect employees to embrace change unless the leaders are already living it.

Three years after the merger, we were still far from building a cohesive team. We hadn't drilled down far enough into the issues and cultural differences that were dividing our people, and even our most senior leaders were still at odds, each continuing to blame the others for holding Lenovo back on the path to growth. As a result, our Eastern colleagues were clinging to their old business practices, and our Western colleagues were importing their own styles and processes from their previous employers: Dell, IBM, McKinsey, and others. The thinking was, "Well, no one has shown me a better way, so why change?" The result was chaos. However, there were a few who were emerging as leaders who were willing to explore alternative strategies for getting things done in this new world order. They were taking action and embracing change in some surprising ways.

Changing Culture Is in the Details

Yolanda noticed that something was different in the third floor ladies' room of Lenovo's Beijing headquarters. All the toilets had been replaced with brand-new, Western-style toilets.

Previously, her office's restroom had had both Western toilets and Chinese-style squat toilets (ceramic holes in the floor flanked by treaded tiles to stop users from slipping). These were common fixtures throughout China, and many Westerners who were new to the country found them challenging. Using them required balance and leg muscles.

By then, Yolanda was used to Beijing-style plumbing. She also knew that while many middle-class, educated Chinese used Western-style toilets at home, most of them felt that the Chinese toilets were more hygienic in public spaces; they feared that they could catch a disease if their bare skin came into contact with a toilet seat. In 1997, Du Jianhua, currently our vice president of the Lenovo China Labor Union, started to replace some of these squat toilets, eventually adding three new Western-style toilets to the two traditional bowls, to make his Western colleagues feel more comfortable when they visited China.

The three-to-two ratio seemed more than fair to Yolanda, although the vast majority of her colleagues in Beijing were Chinese, and she'd heard that her colleagues weren't thrilled with the makeover. Du Jianhua, or "Lao Du," as he is known, had encountered a lot of resistance to the changes, but he persisted.

Lao Du was determined that a Western visitor or colleague walking through our buildings would feel as comfortable there as at any sprawling IT campus in Silicon Valley, a role that he took very seriously. No detail was too small, whether it was the toilets or the temperature in the conference rooms, where Westerners generally preferred a cooler temperature and Easterners almost always wanted the thermostat set at a cozy 22 degrees Celsius (72 degrees Fahrenheit) or above. Lao Du turned the temperature down.

One of his earliest moves was to establish coffee shops on the office grounds. Noticing that many global technology companies in the West, including our own in Raleigh, had coffee shops on the lobby level, YY had Lao Du develop and install Lenovo's own sleek, branded cafés, with uniformed baristas; display cards explaining the milk-to-coffee ratios of espressos, lattes, and cappuccinos; and a selection of Japanese sponge cakes and sandwiches.

Many of these changes were inspired by YY, who bristled at anything that might stereotype Lenovo as "typically Eastern" in the eyes of our Western colleagues and partners. Everything had to be perfect. Lao Du still recalls our boss's irritation when executives from Intel came to our headquarters for a meeting and couldn't get a cup of coffee. Instead, we served loose-leaf jasmine and chrysanthemum Chinese tea—a delicate, aromatic drink, but not necessarily what every Westerner wants to sip in a business meeting. It takes time to brew, and it can be awkward to drink, as they end up having to discreetly spit out the tea leaves and flower petals that haven't yet sunk to the bottom of the cup.

"We couldn't give them something as simple as a cup of coffee. It's not good enough!" YY exclaimed after the meeting.

Our traditional tea service was also distracting and not to Westerners' tastes. So Lao Du arranged for a buffet-style tea and coffee service for meetings instead.

"YY is a sensitive person who cares about people's feelings, and after spending so much time abroad, these simple changes seemed like common sense to him," Lao Du reasoned, justifiably proud of the way he'd helped transform Lenovo China's working environment.

Customize the Playbook for a Global Overhaul

Of course, toilets and tea and coffee services were the least of the internal globalization challenges that we faced. After the McKinsey audit, from 2007 to 2008, all of the more fundamental cultural issues were discussed in detail in off-site workshops, roundtables, individual employee reviews, and senior leadership quarterly reviews. Yolanda and her team designed customized workshops intervention programs, and tools and resources that would suit Lenovo. What they quickly discovered was that there was no playbook for the situation in which they found themselves. There was little that was currently on the shelf that was relevant to developing the understanding of and respect for the differences that we were dealing with at Lenovo, so we did what this company has done ever since it was founded—create something from nothing.

We needed to build a tidal wave of trust in order to change the hearts and minds of thousands of employees across multiple business functions. But we had to be scientific and systematic

Be prepared to come up with solutions from scratch. The global business landscape is evolving so rapidly that the textbooks can't keep up with what is really happening on the ground. Keep an open mind and be creative to come up with innovative solutions that best fit your current environment.

about it, leveraging the goodwill and actions of employees like Lao Du to bring about deeper, broader, and more global changes. This was going to require concrete actions and tools that would address the specifics that we'd diagnosed, such as lack of trust, poor speed and efficiency, and the need for a common strategy. In other words, we needed to come up with a precise prescription and treatment plan that would be embraced not just by our employees but by our executives at the highest levels of the organization.

Beyond Diversity

We needed to begin by redefining diversity for Lenovo and getting everyone aligned around the definition, starting at the top with our senior executive team. We needed to create a common language and get everyone to think differently so that we could begin to leverage our diversity by incorporating the varied talents and insights of our people into their businesses. In her first few months, Yolanda found herself explaining the meaning of the actual term *diversity* to her new colleagues over and over again. Many countries outside the United States do not have such a word. China's population is predominantly from the *Hanzu* (Han nationality) group; it is one of the most ethnically homogeneous nations in the world. In China, women have been officially recognized as being equal in the workplace for the better part of a century, so although things are never perfectly equal, Western concepts like affirmative action did not exactly apply here.

Today, when we talk about diversity at Lenovo, we are speaking about valuing cultural differences in a broad sense, including regional origin, gender, educational background, age, religion, experience, language, organizational affiliation, sexual orientation, physical disability, job function, race, and ethnicity—basically everything that is part of our individuality. Many of our Western colleagues thought of diversity in only the most limited way: gender, sexual orientation, and ethnicity. They understood the term, but they missed the full potential of diversity as an element of business practice. Our Eastern colleagues, meanwhile, lacked the term *diversity*, but on many levels they were already practicing it. So here was an incredible opportunity to redefine what diversity could mean globally, while embedding a true spirit of inclusiveness into our culture. Understood and implemented the right way, it had the power to unleash the talents of our people around the world.

Redefine Diversity for the New Global Reality

As we began to redefine diversity, our perspective had to be much broader than what is typical of more country-centric corporations. Our "diversity lens" needed to acknowledge all the elements that make a person unique, including that person's history, thinking style, work experience, and expertise. It had to be about honoring the many cultures that made up the fabric of the company and leveraging our national and regional differences so that we could better understand our customers and address their needs. This new culture would include "shared values, beliefs, and behaviors" so that we could fully integrate and work together as one Lenovo and be less siloed in our thinking. In other words, we had to build a whole new mindset—a new world culture—that would define who we were and direct all of our actions.

Embrace and Understand Your Company's Core Values

After establishing a common vocabulary, we outlined a set of core values for the new Lenovo. Both IBM and Lenovo had had values, but we needed a set of principles that would apply to the newly integrated companies. Developing this was a critical process that included months of rigorous debate about who we were at our core and what we needed to do differently if we were to win in this new world. Yolanda's diversity team partnered with the HR organization and development (OD) team, which was responsible for defining the core values, as it was essential that our top leaders participate in this process. Having company values is important because it is those attributes that bind together an organization's employees at a global level. We ultimately settled on four core values, with the first three leveraging the history of both companies. In some respects, both IBM and Lenovo shared beliefs, which was a factor in the two companies coming together in the first place. The first three priorities were shared with IBM; our leaders added the fourth after the merger.

Lenovo Core Values

1. Serving and satisfying customers.

2. Innovation and entrepreneurial spirit, particularly as it matters to customers.

3. Trust and integrity, which help build relationships.

4. Teamwork across cultures. This is about making sure that we understand each other, value our diversity, and take a worldview across cultures.

We believed that these core values would lay the foundation for a culture of high performance, a passion for winning, and the ability to change and act quickly. It would foster candor, trust, and acceptance of differences in ideas and experiences. And it would be everyone's responsibility and opportunity to learn new things and develop their skills. We would all be part of an exciting journey: transforming Lenovo into a world-class, global, and *successful* company

Put Teams in Place
Who Will Drive Change

Again, none of this was going to happen unless the principles were fully embraced and acted upon at the highest levels of the company, as it had become clear that our culture clashes and tensions were especially acute among the top leaders. Thus, in order to drive the change, we put a formal project team structure in place, starting with a steering committee consisting of our chairman, the CEO, and the senior vice president of HR. This group was hands-on, taking complete ownership of the process and providing overall sponsorship and approval of team recommendations.

We then set up multiple work streams, which we called "Culture Action Teams," divided up according to the results of the audit and led by the senior vice presidents of the various business units, each one tackling one of the company's priorities.

Lenovo Priorities

- Trust

- Vision and strategy

- Execution and speed

- Accountability

- Capability and innovation

Each group's role was to generate specific recommendations and detailed action plans for these broad categories. What was so impressive is that this work was actually done by the business leaders in conjunction with HR—an unusual practice. It is unusual for business leaders at this senior level to fully engage in defining solutions in areas that are generally considered to be part of HR's role. The HR team would work side by side with the Culture Action Teams to ensure that these plans were not only created but executed, using a color-coded dashboard to monitor the progress of each senior vice president relative to the actions required. We used this dashboard to present the progress of the culture actions, and it was shared in the top leadership meetings. Again, at this level of an organization, it is highly unusual and significant for someone from HR to be on the meeting agenda frequently, especially on the topic of diversity and culture work, demonstrating just how engaged our leaders were about embedding the new core values necessary to improve our culture.

Defining the Economics of Trust

Even before that work began, we had to get everyone in the top leadership team aligned. One of the interventions was a leadership workshop focusing on the book by Stephen M. R. Covey called *The Speed of Trust: The One Thing That Changes Everything*. Put simply, it said that if you don't have trust, it affects the speed at which things get done, and the costs go up (the trust tax), but if you do have trust, you have greater speed and efficiency, and costs go down (the trust dividend). The purpose of the workshop was to increase the trust level on the executive team by: creating a shared vocabulary regarding trust, using tools to effectively deal with team issues, making commitments to trust each other, and getting to know each other better as people by having fun together.

With CoveyLink consultants, we took our top leadership, consisting of about 20 members at the time, to an offsite resort by the beach in California, where the atmosphere was relaxed and our highest-level executives could get to know one another more deeply in a less pressured environment.

The work was not easy. In between dinners and breaks for Ping Pong, there were intense, raw, and honest discussions. Before the meeting, preliminary work was required. Each member of the executive team was surveyed individually and privately. The general feeling, it was discovered, was distrust. Specific practices needed to be put into place to improve how everyone was interacting. Here are a few of them.

Lenovo Leadership Tips

- Declaring one's intent before presenting or communicating in a meeting so that people would not draw the wrong conclusions

- Stopping side conversations

- Remaining loyal to those who are absent from the meeting

- Keeping conflicts within the leadership team

- Sending presentations to each other 24 hours in advance, with clearly stated objectives

These were just some of the many "One Lenovo" leadership tips that came out of our trust workshops. In addition, Western team members were encouraged to *listen to understand* and speak slowly, to make allowances for the fact that English was a second language for many of their colleagues. Our people from both East and West were also advised to put away their smartphones and computers during meetings in order to show respect for the people in the room. Although these tactics may seem simple and obvious, they were necessary in order to get alignment and reinforce respect for diversity within the team.

Build Mutual Respect by Paying Attention to the Details

The tips had to be that specific and practical, because it had become clear that there was too much room for misunderstanding. Beyond language, cultural differences extended to holidays. Many people in the United States felt that their Chinese colleagues were disrespecting major Western holidays like Easter by asking them to travel on a Easter Sunday to make a Monday meeting. But our Chinese colleagues didn't know that this was a critical holiday. By creating a global calendar of all major holidays for all nationalities, including Chinese New Year, Lenovo let everyone at the company from both East and West know that they should not hold key meetings during those times. Today our colleagues even limit email during holidays so that we can relax and enjoy our families on the holidays that are culturally significant to us. Besides showing respect for each other's culture, this ensured that everyone would be included in key discussions.

Many of the global issues we that faced, although complicated by distance and time zones, had relatively simple solutions, but finding those solutions required paying attention and reading between the lines. Jeanne Bauer figured out our protocols for overseas conference calls after spotting a trend. She noticed that when she spoke to her Chinese colleagues at a time that was during her morning hours and their evening hours, the decision that she thought they'd reached over the phone would change over the course of 12 to 24 hours. But if she spoke to her Beijing colleagues at night, it was usually possible to stay on the same page. The reason? When her Chinese colleagues were alone in their homes in the evening, they didn't always have the language skills to fully understand what Jeanne was saying, so they would agree with her even if they weren't sure. But the next morning, when her Chinese peers were able to get in a room together to discuss the points of the conference call, they had more clarity.

"China is a consensus-based society, so I needed to give them the opportunity to talk and translate for each other. Simply reversing the call times enabled them to do that, and this was key to us being able to get agreement," Jeanne explains.

Cultural Training Starts in the C-Level Boardroom

Six months after the trust workshop, there was another major intervention, which we called "East Meets West." Old habits and behavior die hard, and this was particularly true for our highest-level executives, who still had some work to do before they could leverage our many similarities and differences to create a competitive business advantage.

We custom-designed our own workshops and tools, and we hired outside consulting companies C. Forbes LLC and Aperian Global to help develop a host of cross-cultural toolkits and workshops together with Lenovo. The East Meets West workshop, in partnership with Aperian Global, enabled us to go more deeply into the historical backgrounds and foundations of our respective cultures. It was important for people to understand the "why" behind the behaviors. If our executives understood each other's history, it would promote better understanding and a greater willingness to find solutions.

> Develop cross-cultural sensitivity. Take the time to learn each other's background and history, because information provides the why behind the behavior and circumvents assumptions of negative intention.

We began with a video presentation on each other's history, including everything from a map to images of key figures, landmarks, and events. We talked about how the United States is a relatively new country and a cultural melting pot. We talked about its pioneering spirit of self-reliance and individuality, how change is considered positive, and that you have to work hard to achieve the American Dream. For China, we talked about the great dynasties of the past, Confucianism, the strict and highly competitive educational system, the hierarchy of society, and the concept of "face" or *mianzi*, in which you never do anything to embarrass or humiliate another. As the presentation went on, we could see the pride in the faces of our Eastern and Western colleagues when their culture was being talked about. It was a chance to explain who they were—to finally be understood.

We drilled down deeper into each other's cultural values and working styles and how they have evolved over the generations. We also learned how media headlines can influence our perceptions of each other. We then discussed how behavior that builds trust in one culture can have the opposite effect in another culture. In the United States, for example, being your own person, maintaining eye contact, and being more vocal and direct denote personal integrity. But in China, a person of integrity fulfills obligations, maintains harmony, and does what he or she can to meet the expectations of the group. The two cultures also have widely divergent views on what constitutes high performance. In the United States, for example, high performers do what they can to gain recognition or stand out and are praised for their ability to produce quick results. In China, individual accomplishments are played down. Instead, the emphasis is on pushing forward the goals of the team.

The East meets West and trust-building workshops helped create a whole new consciousness. Later, when we surveyed our leadership team, the members told us that these sessions enabled them to get work done more quickly, solve problems more effectively, and create better solutions. The program went a long way toward fostering the mutual understanding and trust that had been missing in so many of our interactions with each other since the acquisition. It was so well received by our leadership team that we made it available to the rest of the organization, especially the members of those global teams whose day-to-day business interactions required them to navigate across cultures. To this day, we use many of the cross-cultural tools and resources for our new hires, and when necessary we customize them for the particular countries they are operating in, whether they're in Latin America, Europe, or India.

Put Diversity into Action

There were many other forms of culture training outside of workshops and classrooms. During her first period in Beijing, Yolanda, with the support of her team, was making this happen not only through her personal interactions with colleagues but also by putting these ideas into action—a kind of "diversity by doing." These were highly specific, concrete steps. Many employees were struggling with the new "global time zone," which meant adapting to a work/life balance that was very different from the standard working hours of 8 to 5. We created monthly tips and job aids to help employees manage their time, meetings, conference calls, and other such requirements more effectively. For our non-English-speaking colleagues, we also offered online and face-to-face English courses, as well as cultural information that employees could study to learn more about their colleagues in other parts of the world.

These small but deliberate actions limited the possibility of misinterpreting one another's intentions, which was affecting trust. As we learned in the East Meets West workshops, the misunderstandings came about as a result of the two cultures having entirely different ways of doing things. Miscommunications led to an assumption of disrespect. We were getting to know each other and slowly beginning to feel like we were all on the same side.

It helped that this process of familiarization was something our colleagues actually enjoyed. Yolanda and her team traveled globally, hosting Culture Roadshows, which were forums to present tips and tools to help with teaming across cultures. Particularly well received were the Culture Toolkits that we put together, with fun activities and useful resources to help employees work more effectively across the globe. Inside the toolkit, which was distributed to all employees, was a meeting planner with time zones, jargon lists for different cultures, and more.

One especially popular form of training that we offered was the East Meets West Gala Dinner at a Western-style hotel for our Beijing colleagues who would be traveling to the United States frequently. Many of our executive leaders wanted to feel more comfortable in an international social setting, so the purpose of the dinner was to teach our Eastern colleagues Western-style etiquette, from how to make small talk at a cocktail party to the difference between a steak knife and a fish knife. Yolanda taught her Beijing colleague about the meanings of dress codes, from business casual to cocktail and formal wear. Our Chinese leaders were thrilled, because knowledge of these protocols and skills—things that many Westerners take for granted— gave them a huge boost in confidence when they went to their first business meetings overseas. Our Western colleagues were also excited to learn basic Chinese etiquette at our Eastern banquet held in the U.S., where they even learned a few Mandarin terms like *Ni Hao* (hello), *Zai Jian* (goodbye), and *Xie Xie* (thank you).

Look through a Different Lens

Many of these differences went far below the surface, affecting the very way we think about problems and come up with solutions. Easterners and Westerners also take contrasting approaches to business analysis. The Chinese tend to think about the big picture first. It helps them to know the structure or framework up front, because they like to see where and how a particular issue fits into the overall scheme of things and how it interacts with every other element over the long term. Most Westerners, on the other hand, prefer to begin their analysis with a specific example. They discuss that one example, or case study, thoroughly and then figure out the structure from there.

This tendency led many Eastern colleagues to feel that their Western counterparts were discussing only one case and not seeing the larger context, while many Westerners felt that the Easterners were less interested in solving the immediate problem. We started incorporating ways to do both: define the problem in a particular case and explain why it was important and relevant. Not only did this make collaboration much easier, it also helped both sides have a fuller and more detailed understanding of an issue, leading to better decision making for both the short and the long term.

There were many ways in which our different styles were creating conflict at an operational level. Daryl Cromer, vice president of the Research Lab, describes the U.S. and Japanese engineering Lenovo teams as highly data-driven, with many of their decisions being based on objective criteria. It's all about facts and process. But the Chinese teams combine this with core beliefs. In effect, they are willing to take more risks if they have a strong belief in taking a certain direction. Therefore, not every business decision requires pages of data and reports.

Immediately after the IBM PC acquisition, decisions began to be made more along Western lines, with every stakeholder taking a position and either having the votes to support that position or not. The senior leaders weren't bound by the vote, but they took the results into consideration. However, our Eastern colleagues found the process slightly odd and overly democratic. Ultimately, we shifted to a more Eastern approach to the decision making, in which everyone provided a recommendation and the leader made the final decision. It was typical for us to sample various models and then choose the one that worked best, gradually distilling and collecting the best practices from all cultures to free and empower our colleagues from both East and West.

Develop a Clear Business Strategy

As we began the work of establishing mutual trust, respect, and understanding, we still needed to define our strategy going forward. One of the biggest complaints that came out in the culture audit, after lack of trust, was the fact that we still had no clear direction. So we set up another task force to get some clarity and build a kind of companywide "to do" list, making it clear to everyone what our main goals as a company were and the road map for getting there. Getting these goals in writing can help everyone get on the same page.

It was a tall order, but it was doable. The key would be communicating this strategy, along with our core values, down through all levels of the organization. We had to let everyone know, through announcements of new programs and regular progress reports, that his or her feedback was being heard and that something was being done about it. This was a way of keeping ourselves accountable and highlighting the progress that we were making. On his own initiative, Gerry Smith, who was running our global supply chain at the time and today is executive vice president of the Enterprise Business & Americas Group, hired an internal communications person to focus every day on what message to broadcast throughout the ranks.

"This was a beaten-down organization, so I was looking for any win I could find," he recalls, likening the approach to coaching a sports team. "Once you start winning, people start believing."

Establish Universal Protocols for Communication

As important as it was to keep up with communication, we had to figure out exactly how and what to say to avoid misunderstanding, because this was having a direct impact on our execution and speed—the other piece of the culture audit that needed to be addressed.

So, as part of our short-term action plan, we set about the painstaking work of fine-tuning the way we communicated with each other and how we conducted meetings. It wasn't just the language barriers that were problematic, it was the different communication styles. Our Western leaders lacked even a basic knowledge of Mandarin, so they needed to be educated about just how challenging it was for a native Chinese speaker to operate in an all-English environment. Conference calls were worse, because there were no visual cues to help the people on each side understand the nuances or true meaning of what the other side was saying. The need to translate also resulted in some missed opportunities for real dialogue.

This dynamic occurred repeatedly in all kinds of different contexts. However, a little awareness went a long way. In a meeting with her American boss in Singapore, Wu Tong, HR Partner for the Mobile Business Unit, listened wide-eyed as he explained the same concept in four different ways. She was taking a beat too long to respond, and he took her silence for lack of comprehension. Finally, she stopped him. "No, I understand; it's just that I don't agree, and I was trying to figure out how to tell you this," she told him, listing the five points she'd mentally prepared in order to further the discussion. They both laughed about it afterward, but from that moment on he realized that he should take a breath and give his Eastern colleagues a chance to respond.

It wasn't just the long pauses that accounted for the different communication styles. In meetings, our Eastern colleagues would often wait for their turn to inject their thoughts, while many Westerners tend to be vocal whenever they have a good idea to share. This can also lead to Westerners dominating the meetings, while Easterners appear to be disengaged. Whether it was on phone calls or during in-person meetings, we encouraged the practice of calling on our Chinese colleagues to solicit their opinions and reminding them that we were eager to hear their thoughts.

Early on, Yolanda became acutely aware of the language challenges that her Chinese colleagues faced, because she was one of the few Westerners to study Mandarin. She immediately understood how drastically different it was from any of the European languages, and she was filled with admiration and respect for how hard her Chinese colleagues had worked to master her language.

Learning Mandarin also clarified some of the root causes of the communication problems. Yolanda learned that there is no word-for-word translation into English—a fact that could lead to some major misunderstandings. When she emailed someone to "request" a meeting, for example, this implied that it was a command coming from someone more senior in the corporate hierarchy and that the meeting was mandatory, while Yolanda thought she was simply being formal and polite. She had unintentionally introduced the issue of power dynamics. But by talking about the offending words and clearing the air, she was able to continue to use them. Their meaning and intention was understood.

Never Assume a Common Definition

Layered onto the challenges of translation or mistranslation was the vastly different corporate jargon introduced by the IBM PC acquisition.

> When multiple companies are being brought together, practices and processes can vary widely. Spend the time to get clear not just about the fundamental values of your company, but even about the seemingly small stuff, like the acronyms each company uses.

Tom Cai, vice president and chief operating officer of the Lenovo Compal Future Center, who was already fairly fluent in English, recalls being completely thrown in a meeting by the terminology and acronyms that were being thrown rapidly back and forth across the conference table.

"What's the DOI in our EMEA markets (days of inventory in Europe, the Middle East, and Africa)?" asked one sales executive. "Can you get me the FGI (finished goods inventory) on ThinkPads in APLA (Asia-Pacific and Latin America)?" asked another. Our Lenovo China colleague felt like Charlie Brown listening to the teacher in the classroom. He was frustrated and embarrassed. It was a noninclusive and lazy way to communicate, but our Western colleagues didn't intend to make it hard for him. It was just that they'd been using that company jargon and shorthand for decades—like most high-tech companies. We fixed the situation, which, we learned, was being faced by a number of global executives. It was a matter of creating a common list of jargon terms, acronyms, and their definitions that employees could refer to, so that we could communicate more efficiently in the future. Again, this was a relatively simple problem with a simple solution, but until we could really get in a room together and lay out all the global issues we were facing, we weren't able to identify something that was having a direct impact on execution and speed because it was blocking our ability to work together efficiently as a team.

Using Lean Six Sigma

To dramatically improve efficiency and speed, we also implemented more sweeping changes all the way down to the factory floor, where they were needed most. Gerry led the task force that was responsible for addressing this particular concern that came out of the audit. When Gerry first joined us in August 2006 to run our global supply chain, he oversaw about 12,000 employees in manufacturing, logistics, procurement, and operations, spread out all over the world. Communication breakdowns were causing inefficiencies that were having a devastating impact on our bottom line. Immediately, Gerry introduced aspects of the GE philosophy Lean Six Sigma, a proven management concept designed to eliminate waste and inefficiencies. He also installed a rigorous daily business management system to help reset plans, targets, and expense structures.

> Empower your people by setting clear targets that they can all get behind, then give precise directions on how those targets can be achieved. This will get everyone aligned behind the same goal, even when multiple locations are involved.

Simplify Your Key Performance Indicators

Improving accountability went hand in hand with the measures we took to enhance efficiency and speed. After the acquisition of IBM PC, the performance metrics for our two main cultures varied widely. In the West, for example, meeting 98 to 99 percent of the budget was considered acceptable, but for employees in China, failing to meet their budget 100 percent was considered terrible. To get more clarity within each business unit of the global supply chain, we simplified everything, stripping down the number of key performance indicators from more than 100 to 5: cost, delivery, performance, cash conversion cycle, and supply management/quality. These performance measures, which were implemented throughout our organization, drove a shared, collaborative approach. They enabled all of our employees to focus on the same thing, limiting the cultural nuances so that people in every part of the world, from North Carolina to Brazil to Huiyang, China, could look beyond their own little bucket and focus more on the overall performance of the organization. Now we were able to look at our processes end to end to see what truly affected our customers.

Eventually, once everyone was aligned on all five focus areas, our costs went down drastically, our delivery time improved, our cash conversion cycle shortened, managing the supply of our components was much easier, and we maintained and improved our industry-leading quality. These moves helped us transform our global supply chain into the competitive advantage it is today.

Be Consistent When Rewarding Performers

These wins also needed to be recognized and rewarded, which involved the final piece of the McKinsey audit feedback that we needed to address: capability and innovation. Throughout Lenovo, our recognition programs or performance measures were in need of an upgrade. Lack of consistency was creating a sense of unfairness, particularly when financial rewards like bonuses differed. People were disgruntled, so, whether they were top executives, line managers, or workers on the factory floor, we needed to define how we were going to recognize people and give them incentives for doing great work. To drive consistency, the compensation and benefits team designed global policies around sales, recognizing our sales teams at corporate events and across the different geographic regions. We also rewarded technical people who were delivering innovative products and patents. We came up with guidelines for on-the-spot recognition, as well as policies on the numbers used for financial rewards and incentives and how these would be presented.

> Consistency is key. Reward people for changing their behavior and focusing on the goals of the whole organization, but keep the incentives and recognition global. Inconsistency contributes to a sense of unfairness, especially when it is tied to compensation, and that can undermine the whole intention.

We also introduced 360 degree performance reviews to measure capability, particularly among our executives. We began by putting our senior vice presidents through this process. It was their opportunity to get feedback not just from their bosses but from their direct reports and others. These reviews identified the key skills that they needed to work on. If there was a lot of room for improvement, and their behavior was not changing quickly enough, even after all of our culture work, we paired these executives up with coaches, who would sit down with them to develop an action plan. In fact, it was through these conversations that Gerry and John Egan, our current vice president of global manufacturing, came up with the idea of the Bold Workout, a target-setting program based on GE's Work-Out principles.

Manage How the Team Comes Together and Executes

All this foundational work was also beginning to pay off in our work as innovators and product engineers. A case in point was Project Unity, led by Dilip Bhatia, our product marketing manager for ThinkCenter desktops at the time.

Dilip, who today is the vice president of our PC Group Marketing and Design, was the first of the international Lenovo team to move to China, in 2006. One of his earliest challenges was the fact that we had two different teams, operating under two completely different management styles, and they needed to converge. Lenovo China was shipping 4 million price competitive desktops a year, catering to the local market, while the global team, formerly IBM PC, was shipping 5 million premium ThinkCenter brand desktops. We were losing millions of dollars on desktops annually. We needed to shift our focus to produce desktop PC products that would stop the bleeding and make a profit for the company.

We did this by improving communication and building trust. By bringing more international assignees onto the China team, insisting on more face-to-face meetings, Dilip effectively became a cultural ambassador, developing a world-class product marketing team that understood its customers, both Eastern and Western. The business was transformed, and it started becoming more profitable with more competitively priced desk-tops and, later on, with greater innovation, including new ThinkCenter all-in-one desktops for our business customers. These all-in-one desktops would transform the face of desktops all over the world, winning a host of awards and becoming the leader in commercial all-in-one PCs.

Another example of how cross-cultural teamwork improved execution took place when design teams from around the globe were able to work together to design the Olympic torch for the 2008 Olympic Games in Beijing. Although we were sponsoring the games, our design had to compete against 300 others for this honor. So we put our best people, more than 30 design specialists, on the project, which took more than 10 months to complete. The team, led by Yao Yingjia, currently Vice President of the Innovation Design Center, was truly multinational, with designers from Germany, Singapore, the United States, Japan, New Zealand, Italy, and China. The designers' experience and specialties were equally diverse, including experts in graphic design, chemistry, engineering, materials, anthropology, art, and history. The team engaged in extensive brainstorming, including game playing and creativity exercises, to help them look at the torch design from many different perspectives.

Working as a cross-cultural team wasn't easy, and there was a lot of tension. The ideas were all very different, and people fought passionately to have their points of view seen and heard.

But there was that fundamental sense of trust, the belief that everyone's intention was to win for team Lenovo, and their mutual faith in one another kept them in a room together talking until they could reach a consensus.

The "aha!" moment came when members of the design team rolled up a piece of paper and envisioned the design: a Chinese scroll. It was to be sleek and modern, yet steeped in Eastern heritage, featuring the cloud theme that is often seen in Chinese architecture, drawing, painting, furniture, and storytelling. It was a perfect blend that reflected our values, the promise and purpose of the Olympic Games, and everything that Beijing and Lenovo's entrance onto the world stage signified. Hence the name: "Cloud of Promise."

Our sponsorship of the event itself was leveraged to the hilt. We'd created a marketing campaign worthy of any blue chip, international brand.

But the triumphant afterglow of that summer didn't last long. By the end of that fiscal year, we'd lost about $226 million. A big reason was the reduction in spending by major enterprises in the face of the global recession. Our Think unit sales, a major profit center for the company, had declined precipitously. We had also missed our profit targets, making this the first time that increased profit in China was lower than that in the rest of the world.[1] We needed to take our culture work up several notches, leveraging our diversity to discover new areas of growth and innovation, and we needed to act fast to stop the bleeding. Sure, our Olympic performance was a nice victory, but, as YY said bluntly, "It wasn't good enough." The real relay race was still ahead of us. Together, we had to learn to run a lot faster.

Lenovo Strategy Takeaways

- Come to grips with your company's core values and build from there.

- Train senior leaders in these values and hold these leaders accountable for modeling them.

- Measure successes and analyze failures through regular benchmarks.

- Establish clear and universal protocols for communication, from meeting etiquette to the use of acronyms.

- Bring in HR to work with the most senior leaders to drive change from the top down.

Leading at Lenovo

From the 2014 Annual Kickoff Speech by
Yang Yuanqing, CEO and Chairman, Lenovo

· ·

To win in the future, we need to understand what made us successful today. How did we become number one in PCs? Our formula for success came from our well-known core strengths:

- A clear strategy and good execution
- An efficient business model and excellent operation
- Innovation in product and technology
- Most important, diverse leadership and our ownership culture

So we should ask ourselves: What did we do in the past that helped us build these as our strengths? And what else do we need to do to be more successful in the future? Today, I'll focus on "diverse leadership" and share my view with you.

Diverse Leadership

The most important lesson I learned from the IBM PC integration is the need for diverse leadership. At that time, I told my team members to be frank with one another, respect one another, and compromise with one another. These three elements were the key for our integration at that time. And the diverse leadership also helped us to win after the IBM integration and optimization.

We have had to manage several kinds of diversity in the past, and we will have to address them again in the future.

Business Diversity

The first is business diversity. When we acquired IBM PC, we kept the two businesses separate for the first six months to ensure that each kept running smoothly. And we also used this time to learn how and why each business runs differently. After six months, we began integrating the back end, where most of the synergy could be captured.

At the same time, we had to deal with businesses in diverse markets. The old Lenovo knew the China market well. IBM PC was experienced in mature markets. These two kinds of markets are very different—emerging markets grow very fast; mature markets grow more slowly but are more profitable. We organized into an emerging markets group and a mature markets group. We ran them separately, focusing them differently: emerging markets on market share growth and mature markets on profit growth.

By embracing the diversity of businesses and changing our organization to best handle the differences, we outperformed everyone else in our industry.

In the future, we will face an even more diversified business. At every step, we need to leverage our strengths. But at the same time, we must clearly realize that relying only on past strengths is not going to be good enough.

Business Model Diversity

So, as we face a diversified business, our business model needs to be diversified as well. We actually have done a good job so far. I still remember in 2003–2004, when we were faced with tough challenges from Dell, we diversified our single business model to the unique Transactional and Relationship dual business model. With this dual business model, we beat Dell and strengthened our PC leadership in China.

We also took the time to understand the OEM/ODM [original equipment manufacturer/original design manufacturer] model and the self-manufacturing model. Now we have built a hybrid model. We take advantage of the benefits of all these models combined.

As our business diversifies more and more, we need to constantly improve our business model and maximize our strengths.

Culture Diversity

And it was definitely no secret that we faced cultural diversity. Lenovo had such a strong Chinese culture, and IBM was much more U.S.- and Western-influenced.

With so many culture differences, we tried our best to respect others and to compromise. Many of you were there and know that this was not always easy!

Let me share a small story: The first IBM/Lenovo AP business meeting was held in Hong Kong. On Day 1, all the Lenovo leaders were in jacket and tie—they were dressed up and trying to show respect—while the IBM leaders were in casual clothes. On Day 2, all the Lenovo leaders changed to T-shirts, but all the IBMers came in wearing ties. We tried to meet each other's expectations without actually communicating or being clear with each other. This led to a few unusual photos that day.

The cultural differences were actually very deep. Lenovo used to be very strict in its culture—everyone had to punch in at the beginning of working hours and punch out at the end of the day. IBM was more flexible. No one punched in or punched out. We did not change immediately to one way or the other. We studied and waited to learn and understand why and how the other side was managed. We allowed two systems for a few years so that the old Lenovo managers had time to learn how to manage more flexible working hours and scheduling. I think you are probably all happy that we do not still have time clocks!

Talent Diversity

To understand how to bring diverse company cultures together, you have to look not just at the big picture, but at each individual and team. This is where we see talent diversity. If you look at the top executive teams from global companies, you will find that many of them have leaders just from their home countries. There actually is *not* a lot of leadership diversity in many major multinational companies.

We constructed the Lenovo Executive Committee [LEC] very carefully. We wanted different perspectives, different cultures, and different backgrounds to be part of our discussions.

The LEC is a great example of a mixed team, with different voices from different backgrounds working together to make the strongest possible decisions.

We also respect talent diversity and leverage people's strengths at all levels of the organization. We now have fewer than 50 expatriates, a very small number for a global company of our size. We hire local talent to run our business locally, and we send expatriates only when the local talent is not yet ready.

What do I mean by ready? First, these people need to have the right business or technical skills. Second, they need to buy into our Lenovo culture: our ownership culture, our commitment culture, and our pioneer culture. These principles must be carried on.

Some multinational companies hire local talent, but still designate home-country managers to monitor it. This approach reduces trust among local employees, and this is not our definition of diversity.

We as leaders all need to understand the importance of building a diversified team, not just at the top of the company, but in every group and every function to leverage the new teams' talents and resources. Listen to the new team members, understand and appreciate the differences, and work together. At the same time, we want the team members to learn and appreciate the Lenovo culture as well. If we do these things well, our integrations will be another success!

CHAPTER 6

Protect and Attack

Lenovo Principle 5: Protect your core strengths with one hand while attacking new high-growth opportunities with the other.

In the early spring of 2009, YY had a job for Gina: to find a new senior vice president of strategy. Although by then Gina had successfully screened and hired dozens of top global executives, including Westerners, this particular search was an overwhelming task. This was a critical position, especially now that we were fighting to bring back growth in the middle of a brutal recession.

After going through dozens of résumés, Gina could not find the right fit, and there was no time to waste.

"So give me a few in-house names," YY told her.

Gina thought about all the people she knew within the organization who had the intellect and ability to look at situations from 35,000 feet in the air but who also knew what it takes to execute big ideas and respond to what is happening on the ground. She came up with five names, listing the reasons why they were qualified. When she handed her boss the list, he looked at it for a minute, shook his head, and said,

"No, not suitable."

Gina went back to the drawing board and came up with another five names. Again, he said, "It's not there yet."

She came up with another five, and then another, and each time she got the same response. YY was always exacting, and she knew that this was a tough assignment, but this was getting ridiculous! Finally, she came up with a list of 15 names. She told YY that these were the last of the best of the internal candidates. If none of these were suitable, they'd have to do an external search, however long it took

"No, Gina, don't bother. I have someone in mind."

Gina stared at him, confused. If he'd known of someone all this time, why had he not told her? She was about to ask him when he finally said it:

"*You!*"

Gina was stunned. She told him that she was the least qualified person for the job, and she did her best to talk him out of it, reminding him that she didn't have the right background or education for strategy, and she didn't have her predecessor's ability to design strategy documents, complete with charts and hundreds of pages of text. It just wasn't her thing. Then she warned him that putting her in that job was too big a risk.

"If even I love to take that risk, why not you?" he replied.

She could hardly refuse. YY knew exactly what he was doing.

YY had asked Gina to take on something completely new and unfamiliar almost a decade earlier, and she had had the same reaction. But she had been up to the challenge. Her humility and willingness to learn had made her one of the leading global HR executives in the industry. Gina had contributed to building a global HR team from scratch, in a Chinese-heritage culture in which HR as practiced in the West was an alien concept. She had reached out to HR experts, attended seminars, and talked to her global colleagues, absorbing best practices and bringing us through one of the most difficult transition and integration periods in our history. Long before our acquisition of IBM PC, Gina had implemented the kind of intensive training and ongoing development of new hires and employees that was seen only in some of the most progressive global companies. So when she said she wasn't up to the job, YY knew better.

Gina's particular skill was her ability to communicate at all levels of the business and, more to the point, to listen. When she asked him how he expected her to do the job of strategy leader, he told her, "The strategy job is not about *creating* strategy; it is about coordinating, facilitating, and communicating the strategy discussion."

Gina accepted her new role as interim vice president of strategy, a six-month post that would give her just enough time to get us back on track. Again, she was playing her role as "the water that runs between the stones." She spent the next weeks and months interviewing the leaders of each business unit one by one, asking them to think about what they believed should be Lenovo's strategy.

YY already had clear ideas about the direction we needed to take. That strategy was then discussed in depth during a series of face-to-face meetings with all the senior leaders. They all got behind it, and it was easy to get alignment because all the leaders believed in the new vision, and the strategy had come from all of them. In a sense, this was true, because our Protect and Attack strategy—the overriding corporate strategy—included a distillation of all the leaders' ideas. But with each one taking ownership of the strategy that he believed came from him, it became much easier to spread the message through all layers of the organization.

Gina and her team made this easy by designing a format for communicating how this strategy applied to each employee's daily work. She also measured progress through a questionnaire that had been distributed before the new strategy was designed and announced. Six months later, almost without exception, people got the answers right—a stark contrast from before, when even the most senior leaders couldn't say with any certainty what the corporate strategy was.

YY knew all along that finding someone who both understood the business functions and could communicate with people at all levels—Gina with the support of her team—was the key to success. YY, like Chairman Liu, is a stringer of pearls, with a sharp eye for who would be the right fit for the right role in our organization at key moments in our history. He knows how to leverage everyone's strengths.

YY had done this when he developed Wang Xiaoyan, our chief information technology officer and senior vice president of services, who created Lenovo's IT and services infrastructure. Xiaoyan custom-tailored the department to our needs, eventually bringing our IT expenses down from 3.5 percent of revenues in 2009 to just 1 percent three years later.

YY made another brilliant strategic hire later in 2012, when he brought Gianfranco Lanci, former CEO of Acer, in to run

Europe, the Middle East, and Africa, moving us from the number six position to number two within a year. Today, Gianfranco serves as our executive vice president and chief operating officer, as well as president of Europe, the Middle East and Africa, and Asia-Pacific mature markets.

YY's special skill is in seeing what people are capable of before they know themselves, in particular how they could complement the team. He made Gina our interim head of strategy because he knew she didn't need to be a strategy expert; she just needed to have the humility to listen, the intelligence to distill the information that she received, and the diplomacy and tact to win over the senior leadership. This wasn't a top-down approach in which ideas were imposed; the strategy came from within. Now everyone, including the most junior employees, knows and believes in our corporate strategy. That strategy informs every major decision, from where to expand factories to the latest phone design.

The Protect and Attack strategy has us act like a boxer, protecting our core strengths—such as China's PC and the Think commercial PC business—with one hand, while simultaneously attacking new high-growth opportunities with the other. We work to expand aggressively in emerging markets and to conquer global consumer and mobile markets with new cutting-edge products.

When our Protect and Attack strategy was rolled out in 2009, it quickly became our most powerful weapon, making us a strong challenger in the global IT market and allowing us to realize our goal of becoming the number one PC seller in the world. It is why we have focused on expanding our product portfolio to include tablets, smartphones, smart televisions, and other smart connected devices, as well as our broader port-folio of cloud services and infrastructure hardware such as stor-age and servers, that are critical to powering the PC Plus era.

Be Unpredictable—It Keeps the Competition Guessing

Protect and Attack is fundamentally about balance—between emerging and mature markets, between leading innovation in PCs and developing new PC Plus products, and between com-mercial and consumer customer groups. It is also typical of YY, a chess master who is always thinking several moves ahead.

As Gina has observed, whenever we have meetings with YY, he is always thinking of new and creative ideas. When someone asks him, "How did you think of that? Did you hear something? Did you read it somewhere?" the answer is always different and you never see it coming. That's why he always beats Gina at blackjack. She never knows how he is going to play!

Gina noticed the way his mind processes information in, of all places, Las Vegas. Every time they go to the Consumer Elec-tronics Show, YY stops in the casino for a game of blackjack, a game that requires great analytical skill and strategic execution, and he always wins. He doesn't bet much, nor does he indulge often, but his logical mind can calculate what cards people are holding.

YY takes the same approach in business. By researching and analyzing marketing trends and the direction we are tak-ing in technological innovation, he keeps coming up with a new way, something better. He never rests on a single formula, which keeps our competition guessing.

That, in a nutshell, is the attack strategy that, nearly four years after our acquisition of IBM PC, we were finally able to unleash in the global high-tech marketplace.

Leadership Changes

There had been another leadership shakeup before YY had his strategy conversation with Gina. A year into the recession, Lenovo's sales were nowhere near our targets. Since 2008, we'd had successive quarterly losses, including the $97 million hit that we announced in early 2009. In addition to the global financial crisis, the trend toward less expensive PCs, including notebooks and netbooks, was putting additional pressure on our profit margins, and big customers weren't buying. But there were deeper internal reasons for our poor performance, and there continued to be some fundamental divisions at the highest levels of the organization.

The widest rift was between YY and Bill Amelio. Although the two men respected each other immensely, their styles were just too different. YY was the long-term strategist who was willing to follow his gut and take risks. Bill was the detail- and data-driven guy who was focused on the next quarter, with an aggressive style that frequently overrode further discussion. It was YY's role as chairman to research what was happening and offer advice. But as CEO, Bill was responsible for driving profits, so he had the final say. In retrospect, each of them learned a great deal from the other, but by the end of 2008, the tension between the two of them was affecting the entire company and making it next to impossible to take decisive action.

Building up brand awareness and getting Lenovo on the shelves of retailers like Best Buy seemed like a herculean task, and the potential rewards seemed too far out in the future. Doing this would require hundreds, even thousands more boots on the ground to get our PCs into all the small shops in all the small towns of North America. It would take still more labor to find buyers, distributors, and merchandisers, doing everything it took to cultivate those relationships from scratch.

Getting into Best Buy would mean razor-thin margins and potentially losses for the first year or two. That's because we would need what is called a "ticket"—a price of entry into a big retailer that would require us to price our PCs lower than our competition. Getting shelf space at these national chains would also require meeting a list of specifications. Our Lenovo consumer PCs were simply not known in mature markets like the United States, and without committing time and resources to marketing our products and building up brand-new retail channels, our consumer products would never be able to gain traction outside of China and the emerging markets where we already had market share.

We could apply our proven business model—our transactional sales blueprint—from China and adapt it to local conditions, penetrating deeply into these markets the same way we did in China. But we still had a great deal to learn about selling consumer tech products in mature markets. Some of our leaders did not see the necessity of our doing so, although half of our revenues at the time came from the consumer business. While our commercial cash cow was experiencing diminishing returns, the upside potential of consumer sales was huge. YY believed in the pit of his stomach that this was the way to win.

The tension between our Western and Eastern leaders was a result of fundamental differences concerning long- versus short-term strategic thinking. Easterners felt that Westerners emphasized short-term thinking at the expense of the company's long-term development. And yet making sacrifices in the present for rewards in the future had been our mindset from our founders' first days in that guard shack. While we needed to recognize the importance of quarterly results and answering to shareholders, we could no longer deny our heritage. Long-term strategic thinking was the strength that distinguished us from so many other global IT firms. Of course, we had to be nimble and react to ever-changing circumstances. The pressure was on all of us to deliver both short- and long-term solutions. But too often, these approaches were coming into conflict, and the reluctance to invest in a transactional business model in more mature markets was a case in point.

Observe and Learn

Not that YY ever shared his frustration with others. He suffered in silence, learning global business practices, biding his time, and doing everything he could to manage his China team, many of whose members were confused and wondering what the future would hold. Lenovo China's consumer technology leaders, stars like Liu Jun and Chen Xudong, felt powerless and, in their frustration, were on the point of leaving us. They knew exactly how to make this work, and they were already proving the concept in markets like India, but they were struggling as they tried to translate what they knew into language that their Western peers would understand.

This was 2007, when Gina was still in Singapore, chafing over the fact that she'd been sidelined and was underutilized, and feeling that her opinions were being dismissed or ignored. It was a bad time for Gina, because she had to live apart from her husband and daughter, who had to go to school in Beijing. In terms of her career, it seemed as if her personal sacrifice had accomplished little.

Although she was ever the optimist and never one to complain, Gina was so upset that she fired off an email to YY, listing all of her concerns and warning that Lenovo would be in danger if the situation didn't change. YY didn't reply (a bad sign), so she became anxious and decided to call him. Gina talked while YY listened, neither agreeing nor disagreeing. A few hours after the call, she received an email.

"I don't want to hear any complaints for the next three months to half a year. Learning is the only thing you need to do!"
—YY to Gina

It was a severe scolding, and Gina began to wonder whether it was time for her to leave Lenovo. But YY wanted his star team to learn from Bill and other Western leaders, as he was doing himself. Whatever their differences, he recognized that Bill was good at motivating and mentoring people and at sharing his global experience. Even when his aggressive style rubbed our Eastern colleagues the wrong way, the best and the brightest of them have always acknowledged how much he taught them. YY also adapted some of Bill's more Western corporate practices, paying closer attention to numbers and near-term results. YY understood that he was in this post to absorb all the information he could about global business practices.

Gianfranco Lanci once described the CEO's job as "like the driver of a Formula 1 car." If Lenovo was the car, YY was still in the passenger seat, learning fast so that he could grab the steering wheel when the time was right.[1]

Grabbing the Wheel

That time came on February 5, 2009, when Bill's three-year contract was up and he resigned. Liu Chuanzhi could see the toll that these rifts were taking, not just on the bottom line, but on the morale of the entire company, and he decided to come out of retirement and become chairman of Lenovo once again. Not that he had ever exactly retired. Liu Chuanzhi had withdrawn from his stewardship of Lenovo to focus on his many other business interests under Legend Holdings, which by now included everything from capital asset management to liquor companies and blueberry farms.

Bill became president and CEO at another company. His departure gave Liu Chuanzhi the opportunity to reappoint YY as CEO and to create a COO position, which was filled by Rory Read, an IBM veteran. After two successive Western CEOs, we had finally found the right balance of East and West at the highest level of our leadership. YY had earned his stripes as a global executive and was more than ready to lead the turnaround. Rory was just the person to help him. He guided us through seven straight quarters of growth before moving on in August 2011 to become CEO of another company.

Streamlining and Empowering the Leadership Team

Now that he was back in the CEO position, YY was able to implement his plan. YY also set about building a smaller senior executive team, made up of a business unit and department leaders, that we now called the Lenovo Executive Committee. The way YY saw it, he was a member of the committee—a participant, not the leader. It was a subtle but empowering distinction, enabling the committee to make decisions as a team.

This was key to bringing about consensus while at the same time streamlining the decision-making process. The previous leadership group had certainly been diverse, but there is a fine line between diversity and chaos. There had been too many captains with equally strong views about which direction to take, and it was leading us nowhere. By trimming the number of top leaders from 17 to 9 we gained more focus and faster alignment. With this newly structured leadership team in place,

YY could move quickly to create the new strategy and reorganize the company divisions and product groups. The pressure was on to work smarter—faster and with greater discipline. This made the success of our diversity recipe all the more paramount.

Rules of Engagement Must Be Modeled by Senior Leaders

Before we could implement Protect and Attack effectively, we had to bring our culture in line with this new strategy through a code of conduct that was based on who we truly were. By 2009, we understood each other's differences, but it wasn't enough. As was true of our strategy, all the culture work that we'd done earlier to establish rules of engagement hadn't gone far enough. We were finally waking up to the fact that culture integration doesn't happen overnight and that we were still very much a work in progress.

The effort to create a unified culture takes time and leadership. It goes much deeper than culture toolkits and global calendars. All those diversity workshops, culture audits, and forums notwithstanding, we needed our top leadership team to put its foot down and say, "This is who we are at our core, and this is how we are going to behave toward each other." It was about taking everything that we'd learned about diversity and putting it into action, enabling the extraordinarily diverse talent of our people to spark the innovation, creativity, and performance excellence that we needed if we were to conquer new territories and product categories.

The result is something that, since we formally rolled out these new practices in 2010, we have been calling the Lenovo Way. Broadly speaking, it honors the many cultures that make up the fabric of the company and leverages our national and regional differences so that we can better understand our customers and address their needs wherever they live.

Of course, defining the Lenovo Way was a complex task because we don't fit the typical model of a multinational that grows locally and then exports its heritage culture worldwide. From the beginning, our leaders rejected the idea that other regions within our organization should adapt to the parent company's business model and culture.

> We have chosen to grow in multiple regions at once, drawing the best ideas from employees in all 60 countries and distilling them to create a single unique culture that is more in tune with the business realities of a more interconnected global marketplace.

This process took months of rigorous debate about who we were at our core and what we needed to do differently if we were to win in this new world. While YY was the executive sponsor of our strategy work, coordinated and communicated by Gina, Liu Chuanzhi decided that it was time for him to step in to oversee the culture of the company.

It was essential for our top leaders to participate. Having company values is important because it is those attributes that bind together an organization's employees at a global level. We had defined these core values in 2007 during our New World, New Thinking programs, but they had yet to be deeply embedded in our culture—a fact that Liu Chuanzhi zeroed in on with laserlike focus.

Our Founder Does an Intervention

Our company's founder and owner, Chairman Liu, was so concerned about defining our culture that he decided to fly into Raleigh for a face-to-face meeting with Yolanda and her boss. Yolanda was now responsible for organizational and leadership development as well as cultural and diversity integration. The topic was so important to him that he'd blocked off his entire day for the meeting, despite the many demands on his time from all the other companies that he ran under Legend Holdings. From the beginning, Liu Chuanzhi has always believed that people drive strategy and culture unites people, so this was right in his wheelhouse.

The conversation, which flowed with relative ease through a top-notch translator, went on for hours as Chairman Liu was brought up to speed on all the culture work that had been done up until that point in 2009. There were deep and candid discussions about the meaning and significance of defining a culture within an organization, the issues we had been facing since the IBM PC acquisition, and the many programs, tools, and interventions that we'd created to address these unique challenges. We also discussed how we were measuring our success.

Then the discussion turned to where we were failing.We talked about the fact that our management team's skills were still below expectations, especially when it came to matters of global leadership. We described how the gap in trust still existed, and how communication at all levels of the company—up, down, and across different business functions—was lacking, as was accountability, which needed to be a part of the company's fabric. Finally, we talked about how we needed better collaboration, especially among our leaders, who were not walking the talk of inclusiveness and respectful cross-cultural engagement.

Finally, Liu Chuanzhi asked, "So what about our core values? If we are practicing them, then why are we having all these problems?"

We had identified what those values were during our earlier culture work in 2007: prioritizing customer service, fostering an entrepreneurial spirit, building trust and integrity, and applying the principles of teamwork across cultures. They were the result of weeks of intense debate among our leaders at the time. But the core values were not being acted upon to their fullest potential.

Strip Down Your Corporate Values and Identity the Essentials

"Do you believe that these are the right core values?" he asked. "Are these the values that will help to drive a successful business strategy?"

The questions made us pause. Then Chairman Liu got to his point. We needed to focus on the two core values that were most critical at the time. We couldn't answer his question immediately. We couldn't say which two had to come first. But that question got us thinking about the issues we were facing in an entirely different way.

The discussion of values made Yolanda realize that we were still very much a work in progress. As beneficial as our early culture work had been, we realized that we needed a plan that would take a more rigorous approach to embedding the diversity of our cultures into our DNA. This was just the beginning. Cultural change is a journey—it doesn't happen overnight. It is an ongoing process of tweaking and adjusting the culture so that it continually improves. Embracing diversity was just a first step, a foundation. But we also needed a plan for executing the culture change in real terms, a way for all of us to behave.

Keep It Simple

So we took up Chairman Liu's challenge. YY and his direct reports in the executive committee along with the HR team spent hours drilling down into the values that defined who we are and that had made Lenovo a successful company in the past. We asked ourselves what were the most critical things for people to do to make our strategy a success, deliver on their goals, and guide their day-to-day actions. Where *should* our efforts be focused?

> After much discussion, and with input from Chairman Liu, we decided to focus on two values that could have a significant impact on our business: trust and entrepreneurship. For a company, trust is defined by *delivering on commitments* to the board, our customers, our investors, and our people. And to deliver on those commitments, each of us needed to demonstrate entrepreneurship and "take ownership" of our actions and our results.

Although the initial conversation within the LEC was about trust and entrepreneurship, we realized that ownership and commitment cut across all our values. Serving our customers well, exceeding their expectations, and working collaboratively on teams that span different cultures—each takes commitment and ownership. Simply said: "We do what we say. We own what we do." That's the nutshell version of the Lenovo Way. It sums up how we behave and how we take action.

As we face new marketplace challenges and as the needs of our customers change, our focus may also change, which is why we need to be able to adopt new ways of working. But one thing that will not change is the Lenovo Way. We all share the same aspiration: to build a culture of commitment and trust. We are fundamentally a culture in which people take pride in and ownership of their work, make agreements on their goals, and execute with excellence. The Lenovo Way guides us, gives us focus, and enables each of us to continue to work smarter in making our vision a reality.

Lenovo Strategy Takeaways

- Effective strategy comes from within—all employees as well as leaders must take ownership if they are to execute effectively.

- Cascade the strategy message to all levels of an organization and make it relevant to each department.

- Simplify and distill your best ideas into a single, embraceable message.

- Since there is a fine line between diversity and chaos, streamline your leadership team so that multiple viewpoints can come together.

- Never repeat your last move—be unpredictable to keep the competition guessing.

CHAPTER 7

The 4 Ps for Business Success

Lenovo Principle 6: Corporate culture is not just a document that gathers dust in a drawer. Keep it alive with specific action steps.

O f course, it's one thing to state what the strategy and culture are, and another to execute them. To make the Lenovo Way culture happen and to deliver on our strategy, we translated the principles of accountability and entrepreneurship (do what we say; own what we do) into a few key actions, which we called the "Four Ps": Plan, Perform, Prioritize, and Practice.

The Lenovo Way Four Ps

- We *plan* before we pledge.
- We *perform* as we promise.
- We *prioritize* company first.
- We *practice* improving every day.

We introduced these Four Ps to guide us through the next evolution of our cultural integration, reminding us how to work together, meet our commitments, and hold ourselves accountable. They were key to helping us operate successfully in the global marketplace. Combined with our Protect and Attack strategy, they serve as our road map, with the Lenovo Way as our destination.

Many companies just take a concept, ship it out wholesale, and hope that it works. But that wasn't good enough for us. We collaborated to make sure that everyone not only understood but believed in the Lenovo Way, which included our strategy (Protect and Attack) and how we were going to make this happen: the Ps.

Jeff Shafer, who was in charge of internal communications at the time, helped to oversee the way this message was delivered. He was hired in 2007 because of his view that messaging within the company needed to be handled in much the same way as external communication. The audience (employees) is just as important as the media, if not more important. A dry memo full of platitudes isn't good enough. "They have to be 'sold' on an idea, excited and engaged," says Jeff, who today is vice president of global corporate communications.

Soon after YY returned to the CEO position, Jeff was with him in a conference room, crafting the internal announcements and speeches about Protect and Attack and, later, the Ps. "He had a sense of urgency about him, but also confidence," recalls Jeff. "There were problems that had to be fixed, and he knew how he was going to fix them. It was very easy for me to believe what he was telling me."

The two men spent hours on the content and wording of the announcements. YY is particularly conscious of his audience and what its members want to hear, and this is a major reason why he has gained such deep trust and respect from both Eastern and Western colleagues. Crafting the message to make that sure everyone was on the same page was worth the time we spent on it, because today, any employee anywhere in the world has a consistent understanding of our strategy and exactly what the Four Ps mean. What they came up with was a clear definition and business examples that show exactly how these principles are put into practice.

Plan

For the first P, planning, YY talked about the importance of analyzing the situation on the ground and coming up with realistic targets.

> To do what we say, we need to plan before we pledge.
> We are willing to make commitments to our targets
> based on rational and accurate analysis.
> —YY

"So how do we do this?" he continued. "I think there are three points. First, we need to understand the background and the current situation, including the internal and external opportunities and challenges. We need to know ourselves—our strengths and weaknesses. Second, we need to know where we are going—to set a clear target that is ambitious but achievable.

We should be neither overconfident nor too conservative. Finally, we need to create the plan. After we set a clear target, we need to break this target down into different teams and functions, set milestones, make realistic plans, and achieve the objective step by step."

YY used the example of our LEC and the process it had used to set targets for the next three to four years. At first, because our leaders had come from such different cultures, we had different ideas about the relationship between budgets and aspirations. For example, former IBMers tended to set "stretch targets." If they did not achieve 100 percent of those targets, 80 percent would be considered acceptable as long as there was a good explanation for not going all the way. Depending on which corporate culture someone came from, a target might not be considered aspirational.

But that had to change, because in order to break through, becoming profitable and gaining market share, especially given the market challenges we were facing during the economic downturn in 2009, we needed a better focus, one that was shared by everyone. So the LEC made our goal to first increase our market share and then gradually improve profitability. All the members agreed that achieving an industry-leading position was the first priority and that it was something that was both a stretch target and achievable, because we were only two to three percentage points away from a double-digit market share. Having that possibility within our sights energized the teams.

To execute, the Emerging Markets Group focused on growing market share as much as possible, while allowing for a certain amount of loss. For the Mature Markets Group, our priority was a return to profitability. For China, we focused on maintaining market share and improving profitability, with the goal of satisfying investors so that we could obtain more funding to further our Attack strategy. It worked. Within a year, we'd turned things around and were on our way to growth on both fronts: profits and market share.

As YY put it, "This clear strategy ensures that every team understands its focus, and then determines targets for each smaller segment of the business and value chain. This keeps us aligned under the overall corporate strategy and ensures that everyone is supporting the overall target.

Perform

The next P, performance, refers to the "do as you say" piece of the Lenovo Way by establishing the process, taking responsibility for it, putting it into action, and driving for results. In order to execute our strategic intent, YY described the six elements that our management team needed to focus on: "an organizational structure that is aligned with the strategy; the right talents in the right roles; the process that supports end-to-end execution; clear targets for each of our functions; fair measurement for each function and team; and performance-driven incentives."

He then gave the example of the rollout of our transactional business model. Before we started the transaction business, we didn't have the frontline system we needed in order to carry it out. Instead, we had been focused on our main business, which used the relationship model to sell premium Think products to large enterprises. In this business, the sales route was to sell direct and through commercial-facing channels. We didn't need to do any marketing campaigns, and pricing was done on a case-by-case basis, using a bidding system.

So we needed to come up with a new structure for selling to the transactional customer and to expand our product portfolio. So we transformed our sales channels, adding more resellers and moving our focus from top-tier distributors to smaller second- and third-tier resellers and retailers. We added several marketing campaigns, and we planned our full year's sales activities in line with this more campaign-driven process. We also adjusted our pricing to address the needs of the different markets. This, in turn, required better inventory control, which we have been continuously improving.

"This is a big transformation," YY told his audience. "We must transform if we want to break through and achieve higher goals. Transformations mean that we do things that we are not historically good at."

· ·

Transformation means change in people,
organization, roles, and responsibilities. It
is not an easy task, but we must realize that
it is the only way to build new capability.
—YY

· ·

Prioritize

For the third P, prioritizing, or putting Lenovo first, YY talked about the meaning of ownership.

"As a management team, your commitment and motivation has been proven," he told the audience. "But we still need
to reach for a higher standard. That is ownership. Really act as
if you are the owner of Lenovo. As owners, our every effort and
every motivation is to make Lenovo a great company. And then
we will not only be successful in our performance, but also successful in our careers."

But ownership can play out in different ways. There is active ownership, and then there is passive ownership.

....

We must proactively take on responsibilities
and be willing to hold ourselves accountable.
We don't wait to act, and we don't complain.
—YY

....

YY also urged cultivating a sense of ownership that balances
short-term performance and long-term investment. "Never
seek only short-term, unsustainable success or profit, and avoid
being shortsighted," YY said. A case in point was the decision to
develop the emerging markets and mobile Internet businesses.
In the short term, this might not seem like a good move, but in
the longer term it would lead to sustainable growth.

YY also discussed the dynamics of ownership in terms of
the whole versus the part. In other words, we must put the interests of the whole company before those of our own business
unit. YY also talked about individual ownership. "We should
tie personal development with company development," he
said, mentioning Yolanda as a case in point.

"She's American, and she had a peaceful life there. But in
order to experience a different culture, and to help the company

bridge two cultures, she moved her entire family to China. She and her family have overcome a lot of difficulties. In the interests of the company, she sacrifices a lot. But meanwhile, she also gains a lot."

YY did the same, moving to Raleigh to demonstrate Lenovo's determination to go global. "Everyone in my family had to learn to adapt to a new way of living, which was not easy. But it also afforded us good opportunities to grow."

Practice

Finally, YY elaborated on the fourth P, practice.

To demonstrate ownership, we should have ambition and pursue improvement. Once we achieve a milestone, we should not be complacent; instead, we should set higher targets.

—YY

To that end, he urged us to learn from the past by searching for the root causes of our successes and failures. We also needed to learn for the future by striving to understand trends in the market, industry, and technology. Our success in building up our mobile Internet business is another example. We had identified this future trend a few years earlier and had begun to prepare through research and development, enabling us to launch our first wave of impressive products at the Consumer Electronics Show in Las Vegas by the beginning of 2010. "All these are the results of preparation and looking to the future."

YY's speech drove home the point that our Lenovo Way culture and our Four Ps are relevant in real terms, going way beyond slogans to shape the way we run our day-to-day business on multiple fronts.

"The Four Ps do not only apply to our culture—they affect our business. They drive our sustainable growth and transform Lenovo into a built-to-last company."

As powerful as our leaders' speeches about culture, strategy, and principles were, they didn't stop there. Everything that Liu Chuanzhi, YY, and the rest of the leadership team did and said telegraphed just how seriously the Four Ps were to be taken by every employee, at all levels of the organization.

As YY emphasized, "Only when all managers really believe in the culture, live the culture, and cascade it down can change happen in their team's daily behavior."

This was a unique approach. Having run internal communications at other tech companies and global agencies, as well as at a major international communications firm, Fleishman-Hillard, Jeff had witnessed several corporate messaging strategies, and the difference this time was clear.

"At some companies, colleagues are dragged into culture meetings and asked to write up three principles for a company's manifesto or credo. They put these principles on badges and posters, and they make them speaking points a couple of times. The principles just sort of languish there and die," explains Jeff. "But here, the senior leaders recognized early on that culture was a big deal. The integration was never just about blending business operations like IT, sales, or manufacturing. Culture gets talked about all the time at Lenovo, and you know that the leaders mean it. It's an issue that bubbles all the way up to the top."

Our executives were critically important to the success of the Lenovo Way. We knew that if they failed to "walk the talk," the rest of our colleagues would never adopt the new values. Never one to ask others to do something he was not prepared to do himself, YY insisted on being the first leader to participate in a 360 degree performance review against the Four Ps that defined the Lenovo Way. He genuinely wanted to know how he was doing, and he wanted to hold himself up to the highest standards that we'd defined for our new corporate culture. Once he had expressed his own opportunities for growth and developed an action plan, his team of direct reports did the same. This was a great example of leaders holding themselves accountable first, then asking their people to commit. To ensure that there was follow-through, accountability partners from our global HR team were put in place to support the development needs that were identified in the performance review. The review itself was adapted specifically to the Four Ps, tracking progress on how our leaders were sticking to and developing in these principles using a "change management dashboard," a color-coded tool that we had developed to monitor progress and highlight the importance of the Ps. Within this framework, to identify areas where functions were less than exemplary, each business leader would conduct a SWOT (strengths, weaknesses, opportunities, and threats) analysis within their function to determine what needed to change in order to best operate in the Lenovo Way. The leaders would then share the results of the SWOT dashboard in executive committee meetings and coach one another, giving feedback throughout the year on what areas still needed work. This extensive review process was part of a three-pronged approach that we used to get everyone aligned and to get the Lenovo Way embedded into the fabric of the company: define the culture, establish a methodology to drive the culture change, and have leaders model the right behavior. Most companies only define and communicate the culture. But when you drive that culture change with methodology and hardwire your principles into people's daily behavior, starting at the top, the culture tends to stick.

The Lenovo Way Four Ps themselves were a direct result of our diversity. We traveled globally, seeking input from employees in all areas, from China and the Asia-Pacific region to Europe and North America. Everyone was asked what he or she thought it would take to make us successful as a business, and the results of that feedback were the same everywhere. It took a lot of work to get the words exactly right, especially in China, where translation and meaning can be two separate things.

The translation into multiple languages had to accurately reflect the essence of the idea but also allow a certain level of flexibility to make it resonate globally. For Lenovo, translation is a demanding task. It requires not a word-for-word translation, which often turns out awkward and unnatural, but a rewriting in another language that is equally powerful and elegant.

When we had the messaging right, by the spring of 2010, we cascaded the concept through training and used the language everywhere: on posters; in presentations; as criteria for awards; on the backs of our employee badges. Yolanda, sponsored by Chairman Liu, YY, and the Lenovo Executive Committee, led this effort, facilitating global meetings to spread the message. It started with our executive committee spending full days in three locations (China, Europe, and North America) with more than 300 executives to share the new strategy and the Lenovo Way. The two are interdependent, and they have been instrumental to all our recent successes.

Getting the official rollout of the Lenovo Way and the Four Ps just right in each market was key—it had to be a demonstration of how seriously we were taking these behaviors. At the end of each session, for example, there was a ceremony in which the leaders were called to the stage to show their commitment to the Lenovo Way, and there was a huge banner on the stage for the executives to sign. At the end of the sessions, the signatures of the executives were collected and posted on the Leading@Lenovo website, so that everyone in the company could see their commitment in black and white.

This event needed to be customized for each location to ensure that it would connect with the audience, and to leave no room for misinterpretation. We spent months in preparation. No detail was too small, not even the hierarchy of the rollout and who should receive the information first.

In every session, at the end, each leader was asked to make a commitment to the Lenovo Way. Everyone wrote his or her commitment on a card; they then came up onto the stage one by one, starting with Chairman Liu and YY, who took the extra step of reading their commitments out loud.

The Lenovo Way events, which included those powerful speeches by YY and Liu Chuanzhi, were a global success. At the end of each Lenovo Way rollout, our global leaders were each given "meeting-in-a-box" materials created by the HR Team team to help them cascade the message, the strategy, and the Lenovo Way until they had reached every employee in the company. Today, you can walk up to any employee—in the factory or on the sales floor—and ask about it. They all know the Lenovo Way and the Four Ps inside out.

Of course, communication and training were not enough. All of our HR and business processes had to be revised to support the Lenovo Way. This entire endeavor was about enabling the delivery of strong business results. To that end, the new values and action plans had to be embedded in all aspects of our human resource planning. Other processes and programs that we embedded to make the Four Ps come alive include:

- Our hiring and recruitment process, so that before an employee even joins the company, we introduce that employee to the Four Ps, which are now a part of the interview guide.

- When an employee attends orientation upon joining Lenovo, that employee learns about the Four Ps. Understanding these principles early helps the new employee become successful in the company.

We were laying the foundation, taking those concepts from the Four Ps and making them operational to the nth degree so that people couldn't run away from them. We changed our HR processes so that people were being held accountable, and their promotions depend on it.

Finally, we used positive reinforcement, linking all rewards and recognition to the Lenovo Way Four Ps. We recognized the way individual employees exemplified these new principles by giving them awards at what we called our "kickoff meeting," which became an annual event to rally the troops around the globe. Our leaders' rousing speeches at this event were a kind of State of the Union address to all of our employees, with tributes and major announcements of our strategies and goals for the year to come.

All these steps ensured that the Lenovo Way was fully integrated into the company and became a part of the way we do business every day. Since 2010, we have continued to evaluate and assess how our culture is progressing through the Lenovo Listens employee survey.

When it came time ultimately to add a Fifth P—Pioneering, to focus on innovation—we followed a similar process, and a survey showed that 88 percent of Lenovo employees now say that they understand the term *pioneering*—more on that in the last chapter of the book.

The Innovation Triangle in Action

All of this was reinforced with the Lenovo Way award, recognizing employees for being role models for the Lenovo Way. Another effective tool was stories, collected by the communications team throughout the organization. Concrete examples were key, because words, however resonant, mean little until there is an opportunity to convert principles into practice.

One example of a success story that demonstrated our core principles at work came from our "Innovation Triangle"— our global engineering team, which includes groups from the United States, Japan, and China—which had to quickly learn and practice the true meaning of one of the Ps: prioritizing.

Having the Innovation Triangle gives us a distinct advantage in the marketplace, because we can leverage each group's strengths. When your teams are dispersed throughout the world, their strengths and knowledge bases will be different, so you can use this diversity to make your products better, with more worldwide consumer appeal. Engineers in the United States, for example, are particularly good at high-level architecture and understanding customer needs, especially corporate customers. Our engineers in Japan are good at detailed design—making the product sleek and light, for example—and they have a strong tradition of doing that; and our engineers in China are particularly efficient and can turn a design or a concept into an actual product very quickly.

But it wasn't obvious at first how all these different strengths were going to fit together. The U.S. team and the Japanese team had worked together for many years, and the strengths of the two cultures were well known and accepted. Many people from the U.S. team had also worked with Taiwan firms as original design manufacturer (ODM) partners. But no one knew what to expect when we started working with the Chinese.

"I am sure that many people thought that they would be similar to the Taiwanese; however, they were very wrong," recalls Daryl Cromer, vice president of the research lab and one of our most distinguished engineers. "Lenovo's team was completely different. They embraced skills that ran the gamut. They had a deep understanding of their customers, including those locally in China and in emerging markets, whereas the U.S. team understood the mature and worldwide markets. They had the ability to rapidly turn concepts into design—they just did it. Their designs were good, but not as sophisticated those from Japan. However, the most surprising characteristic was their expectation of success. Lenovo had known only success—the company had grown at a great rate and had been successful in every endeavor

Understanding the Chinese team's experience and abilities was an important first step. Our engineers had to stop pigeonholing or underestimating each other, instead learning each other's strengths and weaknesses so that they could complement and strengthen what each group had. This is where learning how to prioritize helped. Prioritizing, or placing the company first, means considering Lenovo to be above the interests of the function or team and aligning goals with other teams, breaking down silos, and working beyond our internal structures to get things done.

The necessity of putting the company's interests before those of the individual teams may seem obvious, but in the early days of integration, it was a challenge, because each group had a completely different vocabulary as well as subtle differences in process that caused confusion and got in the way of creating one seamless, productive flow.

"Both companies had a checkpoint process, and the checkpoints sounded similar, but their meanings were sometimes different in subtle ways," Daryl recalls.

A case in point was each group's understanding of what was meant by the "PE Team." The term *PE team* was well known to everyone, but in China, the PE team meant the *procurement* engineering team, which drives component selection and enables manufacturing. For the U.S. team, the PE team meant the *product* engineering team, which supports the product after its development, from release into manufacturing, and provides feedback to the design team about issues that were found after product development. The PE team works closely with development and supports the manufacturing. It took time for everyone to understand the different roles.

The teams also struggled with differences in the checkpoint process as it pertained to product development and other considerations. As Daryl explains:

"In one case, *commit* meant that product definition, resources, and schedule were locked into place. In the other case, it meant that we had committed resources to move to the next phase, where we would lock in the product's definition, resources, and schedule. Some of us were very surprised by a group's willingness to adjust or tune a project after the commit stage, and others were surprised by the difficulty of changing a product after the commit stage."

But by letting go of their attachments to local practices and procedures and leveraging the P prioritizing, the different groups within global research and technology have been able to get into a creative flow that has surpassed everyone's expectations. The result has been a long string of unique products with recent successes like the Horizon tabletop computer (the world's first "interpersonal computer") and our line of multi-mode computers, which includes the new Yoga Tablet, a product with a unique form factor and an 18-hour battery life (more on these later). The team's innovations led to products that won a staggering 61 awards at the 2014 Consumer Electronics Show, prompting *eWeek* magazine to write, "People no longer need to decide whether to buy a tablet or a laptop, they just need to decide which Lenovo device they would like."

Practicing the Four Ps gave us a common language and goals. It was a major turning point, enabling us to build on a solid foundation and finally build up the fast pace of innovation and growth that was necessary if we were to thrive. But maintaining our awareness and striving to improve the way we talked to each other was an ongoing effort. We could never rest in the assumption that our work was done.

Lenovo Strategy Takeaways

- Practice the Four Ps: plan before you pledge; perform as you promise; prioritize your company first; practice improving every day.

- Remember the fifth P, pioneering, which comes right after the Four Ps.

- Disseminate the success stories that show your core values and practices in action.

- Recognize and reward the new behaviors that result from these principles.

- Incorporate the practices in all employee training and new hire orientation.

- Use intensive on-sites for global leadership training.

- Embed the new principles and practices into performance reviews.

- Customize the rollout of the new policies to each local market, so the message sinks in.

CHAPTER 8

Sharpen Global Leadership Skills

Lenovo Principle 7: Commit on a personal level for true cultural integration.

Yolanda's second meeting with Liu Chuanzhi, via conference call, did not go so well. Since he was the main sponsor of our diversity and culture work, being able to communicate with Chairman Liu was key to our success, but that conversation—done in the morning Beijing time and late in the evening Austin, Texas, time—had been full of awkward pauses as ideas were exchanged through a translator and all the nuances of body language, facial expressions, and eye contact were lost. It was at that point, in the summer of 2009, that Yolanda realized that she needed to relocate to Beijing full-time.

Despite the outside perception that China was a hardship posting, the decision to move was an easy one for Yolanda and her family to make. The restructuring of Lenovo's leadership, along with the introduction of a new corporate strategy and the core principles, or Ps, required Yolanda to travel to China even more frequently. She needed to be in Beijing to deepen her knowledge of Lenovo's heritage as well as her awareness of Eastern culture. At such a critical juncture in Lenovo's global integration, not only would being based in Beijing make her more accessible to the executive leadership that was sponsoring this effort—exposure to one of the world's largest and fastest-growing economies would be beneficial for all of them.

Yolanda's sons Cameron and Colton would learn to speak Mandarin and be exposed to the world outside of their suburban Texas home. For the first time in both Yolanda's and Chris's lives, they would have the opportunity to live outside the United States and form friendships with people whom they would otherwise never have met.

Professionally, the transfer would also give Yolanda the chance to immerse herself in all aspects of the culture. Her three-month assignment in the summer of 2007 hadn't been enough, and she needed to be in China full-time to better understand its culture so that she could fully help to integrate Eastern and Western cultures at Lenovo. But going without her family was not an option. Not only did she need to have them close by for love and support, but she knew that they would benefit from this dramatic change in lifestyle. In a global world, with China as a leading economic power, having this experience would only enhance her sons' future career opportunities. Their visit with her two summers before this one had also sparked their own fascination with the language and culture. So the move was an opportunity for everyone in the family.

International Assignments and Job Rotations Are Key to Professional Development

And that's how most of us, both Easterners and Westerners, viewed these assigments. Despite the inherent challenges of adapting to life in a new country, these long-term international assigments, as well as shorter-term postings, were considered perks. We therefore encouraged such movement to advance critical business needs and personal development .

Living and doing business in another country is key to better understanding its culture. We were encouraged to get out of our comfort zone and experience global diversity firsthand. Since we first acquired IBM PC, hundreds of Lenovo employees have been on assignment from Europe to Singapore; from Canada to the Slovak Republic; from the United States to Beijing; from Beijing to the United States; from Beijing to São Paulo, Brazil; and many other places as well. Not only do they learn from doing business in a new country, but they are able to help their teams gain a better understanding of the many regional differences and similarities that make up the diverse tapestry of the Lenovo DNA.

Beyond the personal and professional growth enabled by international assignments (IAs), they are also good for business. Lenovo leaders live, sell, manage, and work all over the world. Our customers also live everywhere, work everywhere, and shop everywhere. We respond to their individual needs with a diverse range of products and services, meeting customers where they live, and it's the wide range of cultures working together cohesively and seamlessly that enables us to be in every home, office, and school around the globe. So having our employees learn all they can about another culture is much more than paying lip service to fashionable concepts of multiculturalism and inclusion. It's good global business practice.

Sandra Wellet, VP and current leader of x86 global integration, spent two years in London heading up the supply chain for Europe, the Middle East, and Africa. By the time she returned to our Raleigh offices in March 2014, our market share in the region had almost doubled—something that cannot happen without great supply chain operations.

Her tenure wasn't easy. It can be surprising how profound, even in a country with a common language, some cultural differences can be.

Little things, such as driving on the other side of the road, setting up utilities, or figuring out local regulations, were hard to adjust to because Sandra was always traveling, leaving her husband behind to cope. We did not have a large presence in London, and all those absences made it hard for the two of them to build a social life as well.

Professionally, however, the benefits outweighed the challenges. When Sandra got there, we had about 50 managers spread across several offices throughout the region, many of whom had ever met face-to-face before. She brought them in for a two-day workshop, where they openly shared business issues and discussed leadership gaps, and Sandra helped them develop a set of leadership principles that meshed with their particular business function yet were consistent with the Lenovo Way:

- customers first

- act with integrity

- deliver results

- make it simple

- people make the difference

The division had been splintered, but through her actions, the managers were able to build a sense of unity as a team and drive for greater efficiency, building more value into the supply chain. When she left, her colleagues in the region thanked her for "giving them a seat at the table." Sandra also grew so much from the experience, learning to listen and be more open-minded, that she is now leading the entire transition and integration project for the IBM x86 server business that we are now in the process of acquiring.

Put simply, the IA experience works. We've found that nothing quite compares to a complete cultural immersion for gaining an understanding of the complexities and nuances of another market. Not traveling for tourism or making a quick business trip, where one conference room or hotel suite looks pretty much like another, but living, working, and playing among the people who grew up there. Many of our executives, both Eastern and Western, have formed lifelong connections with their colleagues, as well as with the many other local people they encounter when they spend a significant amount of time in other markets.

Admittedly, not many of our colleagues have spent time on long-term assignments, and it is not the only solution. Our colleagues have found that even short trips have had a huge impact on their perceptions and understanding, because they are putting human faces to those voices on the phone.

Intense Connections

I learned just how important the personal connection is when I was working with colleagues in the East. In my culture, a lot of my colleagues are friends, but we tend to separate our work lives more. But at Lenovo China, there is a deep, deep connection. That sense of personal loyalty and obligation is intense. That's why the concept of *guanxi*—getting to truly know and understand someone on a personal level—is so important in the East.

—Peter Hortensius

Sometimes it wasn't the differences that we learned about each other, but the similarities.

"That first trip, after walking around Tiananmen Square, watching young couples holding hands and parents pushing their babies along in strollers, I called my wife and said, 'At the end of the day, people here want the same things. They're just like us,'" recalls Jeff Shafer.

International Postings Change Perspectives

Xudong's overseas experience helped him broaden his sense of what's possible. He spent months in markets like India, building up our presence in Asian markets from less than 1 percent to the leading IT brand, with more than 10 percent of market share. Gaining a foothold in these markets against tough odds taught him that anything is possible and inspired him to do better back home in China. He ended up leading his China consumer team to build up our market share from 27 percent (which industry observers said was our peak) to 35 percent.

Xudong's natural curiosity and humor enabled him to excel outside of China. When describing his experiences—even having his car break down on a muddy road in India—he laughs a lot, and the affection he feels for the people he's met in other cultures shines through. Some of his deepest friendships are with his Indian colleagues.

"You need a willingness to explore how people live and think. In India, for example, when they say five minutes, it doesn't mean five minutes. It means hours. Instead of getting upset, you just have to set up a specific time. It's up to you to learn how people do things and adapt, and how to improve things from our side."

Going Overseas Leads to Invaluable Skill Transfers

Of course, what matters isn't just what we, as international assignees, gain personally from the experience. We put ourselves in these postings not just to learn but to teach.

In May 2012, Dan Stone was sent to Brazil as country general manager to help him develop more hands-on, operational experience as a global leader. As a former McKinsey consultant who had taken over the chief strategy officer position from Gina, he was closely involved in the development and rollout of Protect and Attack, and he knew our leaders' thinking on strategy inside and out. Knowing and executing strategy are two different things, but Dan's deep understanding and clarity on how to integrate and grow our business in Brazil produced extraordinary success in that particular market.

Dan was that country's sixth GM in five years. The employees there had all heard the talk about change before and had little faith that anything that was discussed would get done. After assessing the situation on the ground, he found that the company had little in the way of market share, it was losing money, and greater investment was needed if it was going to tap this potentially huge new consumer market and take advantage of Brazil's manufacturing capability.

Dan replicated everything he had seen YY do with the LEC, streamlining Brazil's management and getting everyone aligned behind the same goal. He immediately reduced the headcount from 300 to 200 and restructured the supply team. He applied our Four Ps principles to hold everyone accountable. Those on the sales team kept blaming the supply chain when they missed their numbers, and the supply chain pointed the finger at sales for constantly changing its forecasts, so he made sure that the forecasts were locked in, got clear on key performance indicators, and "knocked heads together."

Dan assumed that Brazilians were passionate and that he'd face a lot of pushback, but he was surprised to learn that this wasn't the case. The Brazilians were more formal, less confrontational, and consensus-driven. The real challenge was winning their faith, which he did by getting them a factory through the CCE acquisition, immediately doubling our market share in PCs in the world's sixth-largest economy, and adding production capacity—something that everyone else had talked about but never got done. We also added mobile phones and televisions to Lenovo's product line in that market.

A year and a half after Dan arrived, our Brazil presence has grown from 300 people to 4,000 in four factories. Production has gone from 100,000 units in June 2013 to 1.5 million by January 2014, and factories that had been operating at just 20 percent of capacity are now full. Doing an acquisition in that market was challenging, but when Dan's local team members understood the importance of having a factory, they gave him their full support.

Building trust with his Brazilian colleagues wasn't easy at first, but Dan quickly learned the importance of face time. Brazilians don't like to hold important business meetings over the phone—something that we'd become accustomed to doing at Lenovo.

But he got around that hurdle by installing videoconferencing between our São Paulo headquarters and the factory sites in Itu and Manaus.

For Families, an Overseas Assignment Can Be a Tough Call

Of course, a decision to relocate should not be taken lightly, because it can affect so much more than an individual employee's career. One of the biggest barriers for Chinese colleagues who wish to take international assignments is the highly competitive Chinese educational system. Taking a child of any age out of his or her Chinese school, even for a short period, could put that child so far behind his or her peers that the child might never have a shot at entering one of the country's top colleges or universities. When children are young and still in primary school, it may be possible for them to go back, but adolescents and teens often need to stay in the West to complete their education once they've been taken out of the system for the usual time span of an international assignment.

As she was approaching the end of her time in Singapore, Gina was given a choice: go back to China or gain more global experience by moving to our North American headquarters in Raleigh, North Carolina, for three years. "Singapore was hard, but to say no to a U.S. assignment, which might be harder, was not an option," Gina recalls. "If I truly wanted to become a global leader, I could not refuse this challenge."

But there was a major sticking point: her family.

At 13 years old, Georgia, Gina's daughter, was reaching that critical school age. But after the ordeal she had gone through at a Singaporean public school, Georgia was dead set against another move. After much cajoling, Gina was able to convince her daughter. Gina's husband, Frank, an engineer, was also willing to make the move after selling his share of an IT consulting business that he'd cofounded to his partner. He was also devoted to Gina and supportive of her career, so following her to Raleigh was never a question. This time he'd be there in person to provide support and get Georgia situated in her new school.

Discovering the Things We Take for Granted

It wasn't an entirely smooth landing. As hard as the Singapore assignment had been for Gina, it was still Asia, and there was some common ground. And Frank and Gina, like most of our Lenovo China staff members who went overseas, were being sent into a completely alien culture.

Gina and her family were mostly left to their own devices when they landed in Raleigh, but they enjoyed the challenge. They had to find their own housing; figure out where to shop, bank, and send Georgia to school and how to get their visas; and do their best given that English was a second language. Gina was surprised at how much red tape there was in the "land of the free." Getting a credit card, applying for a local driver's license, obtaining their social security cards, and even renting a car were complicated procedures. In fact, many basic things that Westerners take for granted were confusing to them.

Even the smallest things were confusing. One evening, stopping at her local Walmart to pick up some groceries, she was spooked by how empty the vast store seemed, and was so relieved to see a woman passing by her down an aisle that she smiled at her. When the woman glared back, Gina was perplexed, until she later learned that she'd passed her too closely with her shopping cart and violated her personal space—a concept that does not exist in China.

Gina was also pleasantly surprised by some of the little courtesies in her workplace, like the fact that people would hold open the elevator door for her and push the button to her floor.

Despite the initial hurdles, Gina started having an impact on our Raleigh offices right away. Everyone still remembered the moving speech she had given soon after the IBM PC acquisition, sharing her passion for and commitment to the company. She got to know her colleagues as individuals and learn about their families; she blended in with the Lenovo community and integrated her own life with theirs.

Transferring Company Spirit

It took some time for Gina's "company girl" spirit to influence her more jaded Western colleagues. A few months after she arrived at the Raleigh office, Gina attempted to import a long-standing Lenovo China tradition by organizing a U.S. version of our annual kickoff meeting. The purpose of the event, as it was conducted in China, was to celebrate the previous year's successes and generate a spirit of teamwork as they looked toward future goals. It was a way of motivating people and building a winning culture.

But the first time she introduced this tradition to the U.S., employees filed into the two-level stadium reluctantly and sat at the back, on the top level, clapping politely as their CEO addressed them. Gina was mortified.

In the three years since, as we've celebrated success after success, however, our U.S. colleagues have been genuinely enthusiastic and engaged at these kickoff events, buzzing with excitement and spontaneously cheering their senior leaders. The last few meetings, however, have been a roaring success, with every seat in the stadium filled, including the front rows, and with standing ovations for all of YY's speeches.

Gina even made a few fans of the Christmas dance performances she implemented for the HR department as the U.S. equivalent of Lenovo's Chinese New Year tradition. It was another way of imparting team spirit. At first, people refused to participate. But then they got into it, spending weeks rehearsing for a dance competition after office hours. The event was a resounding success, and colleagues now ask to do a Christmas performance every year. So, despite her team members' initial protests, the improvement in morale and teamwork was palpable.

It was hard to say no to Gina. Her kindness and openness crossed cultures and made a lasting impression. Even today, Gina can't walk across the Lenovo campus in Raleigh without a dozen people—from the cashier in the company coffee shop to the most junior HR staff member—stopping her for a friendly conversation.

Of course, the experience also transformed Gina, who gained so much confidence and fluency in both English and Western culture that she could regularly stand up in front of any audience and deliver a rousing speech—something that she was asked to do with increasing frequency in all the company's markets, including China, Europe, and the United States. She felt fortunate to have her administrative assistant, Norma Duff-Greenwood, on hand to explain every cultural nuance that was puzzling her, from the concept of personal space to the U.S. voting system to the importance of holidays like Easter and Thanksgiving.

Both the IAs and the Local Offices Benefit from Mutual Mentoring

Gina and Yolanda often got together when one or the other was in Raleigh or Beijing on business, closing down a favorite restaurant, comparing notes on their IA experiences, and generally talking like old friends. At a favorite Japanese spot near the Raleigh office, Gina confided to Yolanda that she didn't feel up to the task of facilitating all those strategy meetings with the executive leaders and their teams. She explained that, like most of her Chinese colleagues, she wasn't trained in presentation skills, and that she would never get it right.

Yolanda assured her that this was a gift that could be cultivated and that success was all in the preparation. She showed her several speeches she'd written, along with presentation notes—little reminders of when to make the transition to the next topic or session and what key words to use. She coached Gina on how to start and why it's important to let people know the purpose of the meeting, the timing, and who is joining. These were small, practical tips, but they made all the difference.

Gina also took courses and seminars whenever she could. Now she relishes the chance to do presentations in English and is completely unfazed when she speaks to a room in which there are 10,000 people.

Living in the United States and stretching out of her comfort zone has built up Gina's self-confidence to the point where she almost doesn't recognize the timid woman who cried in meetings after the IBM PC acquisition. She credits her five-year assignment in the United States, her constant travel and exposure to all parts of the world, and her friendships with close colleagues for increasing her comfort level and developing her into a global leader who can quickly adapt to new cultures anywhere in the world. In just a few years, she has learned more from meeting new people, exploring new places, and coming to terms with the many complexities and nuances of the cultures she's trying to understand than she could have done in a lifetime if she'd stayed in one place.

Gina grew through her overseas experience. In so many ways and at so many levels, venturing so far out of our comfort zones brought to life the ancient Chinese proverb: "It is better to travel 100 miles of road than to read 10,000 scrolls."

Individual Role Models Serve as Critical Cultural Bridges

While Gina was having her impact on her colleagues in the United States, Yolanda was coaching many people at Lenovo China, guiding not just individuals on her team but some of the executives and other employees too.

It was especially important for colleagues on each side of the cultural divide to assimilate personally during this critical phase of our work—introducing the Lenovo Way to the entire global team.

For the kind of delicate, complex, and ambitious culture work that was required, Yolanda needed to meet with her team members in person on a daily basis. As she had discovered on her shorter three-month assignment in 2007, the insights she gained about doing business in China and interacting with her Eastern colleagues were the tip of the iceberg. She still had a great deal to learn about China's cultural differences. She had to effectively make herself into a cultural bridge, and that would take a deep immersion in the cultures of both Lenovo China and the Chinese community in which she was now living.

The surprising mix of the personal and the formal intrigued her. There was a strong sense of hierarchy, more so than in most Western offices, and respect from direct reports ran deep. But there was also a lot of personal expression. Lenovo was a colorful place to work. Choices in fashion that might be considered wildly inappropriate by Western standards reflected a sense of individuality, especially among the younger employees. People put in such long hours that their workspaces became like second homes. Office cubicles in every department were filled with knickknacks, stuffed toys, and pictures. Greenery was everywhere, as were calligraphy scrolls and small items for *feng shui* (an Eastern philosophy that involves building harmony with the surrounding environment).

One of Yolanda's most treasured gifts came from Zhang Kunsheng, our vice president of IT, who presented her with a scroll by one of China's renowned calligraphers. Kunsheng wanted to have the opportunity to reciprocate the kindness and openness he had experienced from his Western colleagues in Raleigh. When they first arrived, he had invited the Conyers family into his home for dinner. After dinner, he challenged Chris to a game of Ping Pong.

That first year in Beijing was tough. The language and cultural barriers were immense, and often Yolanda and her family felt helpless, struggling to figure out basics like grocery shopping, paying the electricity bill, or even crossing the street without the help of a local.

But their efforts were beginning to pay off. This was particularly true for Yolanda in the workplace. Slowly but steadily, she was peeling back the onion and understanding her Eastern colleagues on a much more intimate level than would have

Running Chicken

My Mandarin vocabulary was improving. But my pronunciations were still giving me trouble, which led to some comical misunderstandings. Mandarin has many tones that are hard to detect, especially for those who grew up speaking Western languages, and a slight deviation can drastically alter the meaning of a word.

On one occasion, ordering what I thought was Kung Pao chicken, or *gong bao ji ding* in Chinese, I said *ben pao ji ding*, which literally translates as "a chicken that runs." The waitress looked at me like I was a madwoman. After some back and forth, she figured out my meaning, daintily covering her mouth with her hand to laugh when she realized what I had intended. God knows what she must have thought of this exotic-looking foreign lady when I accidentally ordered a live chicken!   —Yolanda

been possible during a short-term stay. It took time because the differences weren't just between Easterners and Westerners.

Colleagues, particularly subordinates, could be intensely shy. They found it hard to be direct or to say no, fearing that this would give offense, so Yolanda often had to read between the lines. And yet they would make touching gestures, like a surprise birthday party or thoughtful, beautifully wrapped little gifts based on a taste or preference that she'd once expressed.

Her colleagues were touched by the lengths to which Yolanda went to understand and assimilate into their culture, so they, in turn, extended themselves, welcoming her with warmth and respect. Yolanda's assistant during that time, Susan Shu, or Shuxin, was a godsend. She would often assist Yolanda and her family by phone when they were at a restaurant or shop in Beijing and their conversational Chinese wasn't coming across well.

Of course, there were ongoing challenges. What Yolanda had accomplished during her first short-term assignment of three months had barely touched the surface. She still had a great deal to learn. Now that she was working in Beijing full-time (this time she would complete a three-year assignment), she was no longer a foreign guest; she was one of them, and she had less room for error when it came to things like learning and correctly pronouncing the names of hundreds of her Chinese colleagues.

Everyone knew her. There was no one else who looked like Yolanda at the Lenovo headquarters. That made for a few awkward moments when individuals whom she'd met before would greet her in the hallway and Yolanda couldn't remember their names.

With the help of her staff, Yolanda created a cheat sheet, listing the names of everyone she came into regular contact with, writing out the phonetic pronunciations and noting personal details about them that could jog her memory at meetings and workshops. Susan included pictures of the employees on Yolanda's team and tested her on their names before any town hall meetings—one of the many things that she did to help Yolanda acclimate.

Yolanda also scoured the internal email database to confirm that she was matching the right name to the right person, only to be thrown off when she realized that most employees based their email addresses on their Chinese names, not on the English names that they had picked and used to introduce themselves to Westerners.

As Yolanda's Chinese colleagues watched how hard she was working to assimilate to and to respect their culture, they began to reciprocate, emulating her behavior and seeking out her advice and coaching on a number of topics, including work/life balance issues. Some executives and employees throughout the organization would ask her advice on everything from proper etiquette when a colleague lost a loved one to tips on how to lead a project or how to give feedback in a way that was constructive and encouraging, not demeaning. She even coached them on how to make small talk in business meetings.

Yolanda broke through some of the office hierarchy by being approachable and keeping her office door open, making employees at all levels feel more comfortable with her and willing to seek her out for one-on-one meetings. They learned that it was possible to be both informal and powerful.

Yolanda particularly influenced the women in her office. In Chinese culture, there is a tendency to view trying to balance being a wife and mother with work as a sign of being less capable, so when Yolanda won her Working Mother of the Year award in 2009, many people in the Beijing office viewed it with cynicism. That changed when they saw that she was delivering results at work and still maintaining a fulfilling family life.

In China, it's common for expatriates to go through several nannies, cooks, and drivers during their international assignments, but Yolanda stayed committed to the same staff members throughout her stay and her coworkers saw the way she treated her support team at home as a sign of affection for the people of China and their culture.

These were just a few examples of how having an international assignment in China can deepen the *guanxi* that is so essential to living and doing business in the East, or indeed during any international assignment. Truly, nothing can replace the impact of personal relationships and face-to-face communication for deepening your understanding of the global workplace.

Lenovo Strategy Takeaways

- Leverage long-term international assignments, short-term assignments, and job swapping to develop global skills.

- Dealing with a little red tape can be a good thing. Overcoming even the simplest IA challenges leads to professional growth.

- A personal presence can have a powerful ripple effect on the workplace.

- Learn globally in order to improve locally. True global leaders bring their experiences home with them.

- The more you learn about another culture, the more you realize you don't know.

CHAPTER 9

The 5th P: Pioneer New Products and Conquer New Frontiers

Lenovo Principle 8: Be pioneers; be aggressive and quick to adapt to the rapidly evolving landscape of global technology.

On April 30, 2014, at a black-tie gala in San Francisco, YY stepped up onto the podium to accept one of the highest honors available to anyone in an industry that thrives on innovation: an Edison Achievement Award. Inspired by Thomas Edison, these awards recognize innovation, creativity, and ingenuity in the global business world. In his acceptance speech to the crowd of academics and business leaders in product development, design, engineering, science, and medicine, YY shared some thoughts about innovation.

....

We recognize that true innovation is not just about one invention, but about continually taking risks by making big bets to help define whole new categories of products and experiences. It must be part of your business model, your strategy, and your culture. This is how we make innovation a true competitive advantage.

—YY

....

The award was a huge moment of recognition for us. YY, who was the first Asian ever to receive the award, was being honored alongside Elon Musk, CEO and chief architect of Tesla Motors and CEO/CTO of SpaceX.

The Edison Awards were the exclamation point on a deliberate strategy of cutting-edge innovation that has been our focus ever since we introduced the Fifth P of our core principles in 2012: *pioneering*.

Pioneer: Expand Beyond Core Businesses and Capture New Customers

Pioneering means innovation with the goal of meeting the needs of a diverse and rapidly changing global marketplace. Our success in developing hundreds of award-winning new products is a concrete example of this principle. We are continually innovating in all product and service categories, and this is earning us all kinds of recognition and honors around the world.

The Lenovo Way Pioneering Strategy

1. **Ask questions.** We value conflicting views and opinions to encourage new and better ways of doing things. We ask *why*, *why not*, and *what if* in order to challenge one another, our assumptions, and our current thinking.

2. **Observe the world.** We observe the world around us carefully in order to gather new insights and ideas. We look broadly, both internally and externally, to seek new information and new ways of thinking.

3. **Experiment and test.** We actively experiment and test our ideas, gathering data before we make a decision. We take calculated risks to explore new opportunities.

4. **Network for diverse ideas.** We seek people who are diverse in both background and perspective in order to find new ideas. We colloborate with one another and embrace better ways of doing things.

5. **Connect ideas.** We take the time to think and foster creative solutions by putting ideas together in new and unusual ways. We anticipate the future in order to discover new opportunities.

The Lenovo pioneering prinicple is not limited to R&D and product development. We also encourage and recognize new ideas from all of our employees in every business function.

In HR, Gina inspires her HR team members to be pioneers. In town hall meetings, she poses these questions:

- When you do talent acquisition, do you use new social media (like Facebook, LinkedIn, WeChat, and others) to find potential candidates?

- Do you keep in frequent contact with the talent on a regular basis instead of only when we have an opening?

- Do you make an effort to familiarize yourself with the latest technologies and become part of the new technology circle?

Posing these challenges to our HR team has made us more pioneering, which has led to business success. Our China talent acquisition team, for example, has been exploring new ways of recruiting, using a WeChat platform in order to post Lenovo's open positions and provide referring services. Our HR business partner team has also been proactive in coming up with new approaches, visiting other mobile Internet companies to learn ways of enhancing the customer experience.

This pioneering spirit has been largely responsible for our success as we have grown beyond our original core PC business. In the first fiscal quarter of 2013–2014, Lenovo became number one in global PC sales, and we also saw shipments of smartphones and tablets surpass those of PCs for the first time. By the end of the 2014 fiscal year, smartphone and tablet sales had more than doubled from the previous year and now make up 15 percent of our sales—and this number is growing fast.

We have fostered the Edison ideals at Lenovo with what we call a pioneering culture. This means that we reward innovation and risk taking in every function throughout our company. Every function, every team, and every person is encouraged to drive innovation. Whether they are big or small innovations does not matter—having the pioneering spirit in every part of the company is what is most important.

To win in the long term, we must never stop being innovative. Our customers, our partners, our investors, and our employees demand that we continue to innovate. This is not an option. It is a requirement if we are to win the future.

—YY, in his Edison Award acceptance speech

Entering the PC+ Era

The PC+ era takes us beyond being the number one PC seller in the world to the world of tablets, smartphones, servers, and Internet services.

Not only was YY himself recognized that evening, but two of our products also won distinctions: the Gold Edison Award for innovative computing solution for our Yoga tablet and a Silver Edison Award for our IdeaCentre Horizon Multimode Table PC in the computer and entertainment category.

The Yoga tablet was two years in the making. It was conceived by Yao Yingjia, one of our top design gurus. Yao approached the design as a consumer because he was personally frustrated by the unnatural feel of existing tablets; when he was trying to read from them, he found them clumsy and heavy. He decided that the Yoga version should have multiple modes, including a kickstand so that the device could be propped upright for viewing movies. A frequenter of long-haul flights, like so many of our colleagues, he was also determined that the Yoga tablet should have more than enough battery power for extensive travel.

The Yoga was one of several award-winning products we have been aggressively rolling out, including our IdeaPad Yoga laptop, a thin, light notebook PC with a unique screen that flips 180 degrees to become a tablet, and Horizon, our interactive tabletop PC, at events like the Consumer Electronics Show in Las Vegas, where our product lineup won a record-breaking 61 awards in 2014.

Our Yoga tablet push was just one of many ways in which we were expanding beyond the PC. Smartphones were becoming another key part of our PC+ arsenal, but we needed to make up a lot of lost ground. Very reluctantly, YY had watched Lenovo shed its mobile phone business in 2008; the leadership team at the time had sold the business for about $100 million. But when he returned as CEO in 2009, one of his first bold moves was to buy it back. By the end of 2013, we were already the second-largest smartphone vendor in the world's largest smartphone market, China, surpassing Apple and several other Chinese brands.

This was no small victory. China has 1.2 billion mobile phone users and 500 million Internet users, according to China's Ministry of Industry and Information Technology and the

China Information Technology Expo,[1] with domestic shipments of smartphones expected to reach 377 million by 2016. That means that dozens of companies, both Chinese and global, are competing for a slice of this lucrative market, where consumers already have a wide range of choices, from feature-rich to low-cost devices, because China is also where half of the world's mobile phones are manufactured.

We had to work hard to regain the ground that we had lost in 2008. In the two years that we weren't in the phone and tablet business, Apple had launched the iPhone and started the mobile Internet revolution. Our LePhone, unveiled in 2010, was a slightly bulky device with a clamshell keyboard cover and was one of our first fumbling efforts in the phone category.

Dissatisfied with our phones' sales performance, and realizing that the LePhone could never compete with Apple, our star of consumer sales, Liu Jun, who today is EVP of the Mobile Business Group, took over the mobile Internet division, leading our innovation and design people to respond to rapidly changing consumer tastes, rewarding innovation, and leveraging their insights on local market tastes.

Under his leadership, our PC+ division has focused on developing a broad range of competitively priced, Android-powered smartphones, ranging in price from $130 to close to $400. Chinese consumers upgrade their phones frequently, seeing them as fashion accessories, like the season's "it" shoe or handbag, so the greater the number of more reasonably priced alternatives that are available, the higher the sales turnover.

In order to build capacity for the expanded product category, in May 2012 we invested $800 million in an integrated mobile device facility in Wuhan City in central Hubei province—

an industrial base for the research, development, production, and sales of our PC+ products.[2]

In January 2014, we also launched our high-end Android smartphone, the Vibe Z, priced at $549, to gain a foothold in the U.S. and other mature markets. A personal favorite of ours, its sleek 7.9-mm design has a high-resolution screen, a 13-megapixel camera, 16 gigabytes of internal storage, and plenty of power; we've been inspired to ditch *our* iPhones, too. What people seem to love most about the Vibe Z is the size of the screen, which also comes in 6-inch (what we call a "phablet"), 4.7-inch, and 5-inch sizes. In China, women prefer the larger screens to make their faces look smaller and appear more beautiful— one of many cultural details that our design engineers take into account when they are producing for a particular market.[3]

In smartphones, we have continued our strong growth worldwide, led by our success in emerging markets. In China, we continue to have a firm number two position. Outside of China, we have seen strong growth as we expanded to 26 markets, and we have a double-digit share in multiple markets already. Overall, we grew almost 60 percent year over year and hit our stretch target of 50 million units. We are currently the number four smartphone player in the world.

·······················

I'll be very clear: our aspiration is someday to be
number one in the mobile space. I know it sounds crazy,
but even five years ago, if I had said we'd be number
one in PCs, people would have said we were crazy.[4]
—J. D. Howard, Lenovo VP in charge of our smartphone
business outside of China, to the *New York Times*

·······················

Attack with Bold New Marketing Strategies

In order to achieve our goals, we needed to do more to get the word out about our innovative products, so we applied our pioneering principle to our marketing strategy. Hiring the actor and IT entrepreneur Ashton Kutcher to help design and launch the Yoga tablet was one example. Ashton is well known in the world of social media and technology, and we felt that he would be a great fit for our team—and that he would further extend our reach to a key demographic.

We needed to get more aggressive in our branding and our marketing, just as we were going into attack mode with our new product lines and our market expansion. In the four years since YY had retaken the reins, we'd laid the foundation, turned the company around, and become a market leader. Internally, our integration and strategy work had built up a strength and a confidence that we were now projecting outward. But there was still a disconnect between our breathless pace of corporate growth and our reputation outside of China, which was virtually nonexistent.

Our television advertising in the United States was minimal, with no more than a flash of our name on the screen in ads featuring our Yoga PC hardware and touch screen for Microsoft's Windows 8. We'd done some advertising with NBA star Kobe Bryant for the K900 smartphone, but that was more for the Asian and Chinese markets, where basketball is an obsession and an association with a known U.S. star gave us even more street cred with our consumers. But in the United States, the largest sponsorship deal that we'd ever done was with the NFL in 2012, when we became its Official Laptop, Desktop, and Workstation Sponsor. This helped a little with the 18- to 35-year-old male demographic, but it was hardly enough to turn us into a household name.

Partnerships and Acquisitions Increase Our Global Footprint

We've taken a diverse, multipronged approach to growing a global company. Product innovation and creative marketing strategies are two prongs of our attack strategy, but so is our pioneering approach to acquisitions. With our Lenovo Way blueprint for cultural integration firmly embedded in our corporate DNA, we've moved on to buy or form joint venture partnerships with multiple businesses, adding yet more ingredients to our cultural mix.

Since 2010, we've added a PC and laptop factory in Hefei, China, through our partnership with Taiwanese PC assembler Compal; acquired a ThinkPad production facility in Whitsett, North Carolina; invested $1.3 billion in electronics firms in Japan through a joint venture with NEC; bought a German company, Medion; and acquired a facility in Brazil with the purchase of CCE, a leading consumer electronics firm in the world's third-largest PC market.

These investments have increased our manufacturing presence across all four screens (PC, tablet, smartphone, and television); boosted our overall strengths in innovation, product portfolio, and supply chain resources; and greatly enhanced our distribution across three markets. The acquisitions gave us the added advantage of moving more production in-house. At the time of writing, about 30 percent of our capacity was in-house, with plans to increase that to about 50 percent in the near future. As YY says:

> If [companies] don't do in-house development, they lose the spark of innovation. We don't want to be that type of company.[5]

September 2012 was an especially busy month for us. In addition to buying patents from NEC, we agreed to acquire Stoneware, our first software company, based in Carmel, Indiana, in order to gain access to new technology and the company's cloud-computing services. Although it's a small company, with just 67 employees, the move was another important step in our leadership's long-term strategy. A large and growing part of our mobile business comes from commercial customers, but those customers need security solutions that are airtight—an important new focus for us.

Our joint venture with EMC, announced at about the same time, offers similar long-term data storage solutions for small to medium-size businesses that don't have the budgets of larger commercial enterprises but still need the security.

Leveraging Big Blue—Again

At our 2014 Spring Gala, we announced another historic acquisition—we would be going back to Big Blue to purchase its x86 server business unit for $2.3 billion (a deal that, as we write this, has yet to be finalized). Nine years after our acquisition of IBM

PC, it would be the largest acquisition in our history, bringing in $4.6 billion in additional revenue and adding about 7,500 new employees from IBM's low-end server division.

This acquisition would be a perfect fit for our Protect and Attack strategy, both accelerating our moves to expand beyond the PC and strengthening our core global PC business by enabling Lenovo to provide our commercial customers worldwide with more complete end-to-end solutions. The deal would grow our existing x86 server business immediately, lifting us from number six in the global x86 market to number three, with a 14 percent share.

The investment would also significantly improve our profitability over time. The combination of x86 equipment and maintenance services could generate pretax margins that are much higher than those in our PC business. Higher profits would allow more investment, enabling us to be bigger, bolder, and more aggressive in attacking the PC+ space globally. Not only would we have the world's leading PC business— we would now have a top-three server business and the fastest-growing PC+ businesses in the industry.

The acquisition would also enable us to provide our commercial PC customers with better back-end infrastructure and give them the level of service and support that they had been asking for.[6] Globally, other potential customers could include server farms for mobile devices. Overall, it was the kind of deal that could bring us quick gains without miring us in too many integration issues. It would give us the scale, capability, and knowledge that IBM is known for.

Our IBM partners were also relieved, because we were a known entity. What the company might have dreaded nine years ago, it now welcomed. We'd already proved this model; we had successfully integrated IBM PC, turning that flagging business into a flourishing one and going to enormous lengths to ease our IBM PC colleagues into the new corporate structure.

There was no doubt that we would be able to repeat that history. In fact, since there was little overlap in our businesses outside China, we had reason to believe that this integration could happen more smoothly than the PC integration did.

Leapfrog over the Competition

On January 29, 2014, we announced another historic acquisition. When we got the memo, we were excited, but overwhelmed—in much the same way that Gina and our Lenovo China veterans must have felt when the IBM PC acquisition was announced. Here's what YY told us:

> We will announce today that Lenovo is acquiring Motorola Mobility, and the Moto G, Moto X, and DROID smartphone brands. Taken together [with the IBM server deal], these two deals will help accelerate Lenovo's position as the true leader in the PC Plus era. As you can see, we are moving very quickly in the marketplace, outpacing our competitors and positioning ourselves for continued industry leadership and future growth.
>
> Our acquisition of Motorola Mobility allows us to move rapidly into new markets, with Motorola's established

brands and a portfolio of over 2,000 patents, and the engineering skills and talents of a well-known smartphone supplier. Our two companies are a perfect fit, and we are confident that we can turn this business into a profitable market leader.

We are speaking with the media today about this acquisition and tomorrow will be meeting in Chicago with the employees of Motorola Mobility based there, around 3,000 of whom will be joining Lenovo. I know you will agree that this is a milestone development for our company, and will do all that you can to welcome our new colleagues into Lenovo. We have a unique challenge ahead of us, but I am confident that you, the leadership team of Lenovo, are ready to accept this challenge and continue winning in these exciting new markets. This is a time in the history of our company in which we can all be very proud, yet there is much to be done. I am confident that this team is up to the task.

—YY

This was huge. The acquisition, the largest technology deal by a Chinese company, would help us quickly close the gap with Apple and Samsung and would accelerate our entry into Western Europe, Latin America, and the United States, where Motorola was already number three in smartphone sales. It was a perfect complement: Motorola was strong in Western markets, where we were still less well known, and it was established in mobile phones, where we were only just emerging. As one analyst told Reuters in the news coverage of the deal,

"Using Motorola, just as Lenovo used the IBM ThinkPad brand, to gain quick credibility and access to desirable markets and build critical mass makes a lot of sense."[7]

These acquisitions have been skillfully led by Wong Wai Ming, our EVP and CFO. A former banker with a sharp eye for the details of a deal and a deep sense of industry trends, he has consistently extracted the best terms for our strategic acquisitions, which are keys to the success or failure of such deals.

Protect and Cultivate the Home Turf

Make no mistake: while we were rapidly moving beyond PCs, we were still also a PC company. Despite a worldwide decline in PC sales in the industry overall, we have maintained our revenues, and we have continued to push into new markets. We were largely responsible for introducing millions of people in emerging markets to the computing age. It's what we are known for, and it's a big reason why our brand is so trusted in markets like China, Russia, India, and the Asia-Pacific region.

As Peter Hortensius told the *New York Times* recently, referring to the approximate annual sales in the global PC market: "The PC is *not* going to go away tomorrow. Two hundred billion dollars is a big pie, and we think we can get a bigger piece of it."[8]

There are still new PC markets to conquer, even in China. As Chen Xudong points out, our aggressiveness in attacking lower-tier cities and towns in China has given us the edge. There are Lenovo stores in up to 40 percent of towns, but that leaves half of the hinterlands where we could still sell computers.

To make inroads, we're selling more affordable all-in-one desktops, with all the components located in the monitor to save space in small Chinese homes.

We make products specifically to appeal to rural Chinese consumers, including a "wedding computer," decorated in auspicious red and sold with the tagline, "Lenovo wedding computers, one step to a happy life." We take the same aggressive approach to deeply penetrate markets like India and Russia, which is why we have been less affected by the global downturn in PC sales.

Our leaders believe that the PC market isn't going away anytime soon. Most people still work on laptops and desktops. And it's because of our strength in PCs that we are more competitive in tablets and smartphones than many of our Chinese competitors. When our PC customers in these rural and emerging markets are ready to go to a tablet or upgrade to a smartphone, they already trust our brand. Our PC design and manufacturing capabilities can also be transferred to mobile devices. We have the innovation, the production capacity, and the resources to include powerful storage and cloud-computing services in our mobile devices. Put simply, our PC+ products can do more, thanks to our deep and unrivaled knowledge of PC technology.

Evolve and Reorganize When Necessary

The other thing about Lenovo that will never change is the fact that we will always be changing. We've made mistakes and taken wrong turns, but over the last three decades, we have never once stopped our forward motion, and this constant state of evolution has required us to adapt swiftly. We therefore announced another major corporate reorganization at the start of 2014. As of April 1, 2014, we would split into three new and distinct business groups:

- PC, including the Lenovo and Think brands. This group will ensure that we continue to innovate, drive profits, and expand our lead in our core PC business worldwide.

- Mobile, including smartphones, tablets, and smart TVs. This group will make Lenovo a profitable global player in smartphones and tablets and will develop our smart TV business—our fastest-growing segments.

- Enterprise, including servers and storage. The goal of this group is to aggressively build a new and fast-growing profit engine in our enterprise business, focusing on our business customers, where we already have a solid foundation.

A year earlier, we had split into two major business groups: the Think Business Group, established to sell our more business-friendly premium products to consumers and enterprises, and our Lenovo Business Group, which concentrated on selling PCs, tablets, smartphones, and smart TVs to our more mainstream consumers.

The units were led by Peter Hortensius and Liu Jun, respectively. With these latest changes, Gerry Smith, EVP of the Americas Group, would lead the Enterprise Business Group. Once the latest IBM deal was completed, our head of European operations, Gianfranco Lanci, would head up our PC Business

Group, while Liu Jun would become EVP of Lenovo and president of the Mobile Business Group, with more focus on smartphones and tablets. Peter Hortensius, meanwhile, would become our chief technology officer.

These changes took place in response to YY's recognition that as the PC market matures, new and stronger sources of growth must come from our enterprise businesses, to which the proposed IBM acquisition would be the perfect complement, and our mobile product line, which was greatly enhanced by the Motorola deal.

With Each New Acquisition, the Integration Process Begins Again

As exciting as the news was, our heads were spinning. We were facing another huge global integration process in addition to the ongoing work of merging Medion, Stoneware, NEC, CCE, and our other earlier acquisitions into our existing culture. As we have learned, a deal isn't a success until the people are on board, and that takes time, effort, and investment.

Since our first acquisition of IBM PC, we have always been globally diverse, but never to the degree that we are now, and certainly not in the kind of interconnected way with which we approach our business today. Day to day, it's not possible to work at Lenovo and not communicate with at least one of our team members in a different time zone or on a different continent. There's a cross-border flow that finally feels natural.

We can work with and talk to one another from anywhere in the world.

As we have made investment after investment, the elements of the Lenovo culture are no longer primarily limited to the United States and China. Unlike other global companies, we have no single headquarters. We can't even say that we are based in Beijing and Raleigh, because we have huge design centers in the United States, Japan, and China; factories in Brazil, India, Mexico, and the United States; and call centers in eastern Europe and Argentina.

It no longer suffices to say simply that we are a multinational company, either. As a cover story in *Bloomberg Businessweek*[9] described us, we are a next-generation global enterprise that is diverse, networked, and polycentric. We leverage a network of people for ideas and creation, and the intersection of those people is how we get things done. We do things wherever it makes sense, and we view the world as a broad place. If we have the right facility or setup, we use it. Our diversity is now a fact of life, not something that is driven by an HR requirement, and we benefit from it in concrete ways. Every chipset, keyboard, and high-resolution screen is being manufactured in a different location, conceived, developed, and marketed by individuals from more than 40 different nationalities.

We are no longer a "tale of two cultures"; instead, we are a complex story involving dozens of different languages and ways of thinking. And the pending approval of our latest acquisitions will only reinforce how global we have become as we add another 11,000 people from 50 to 60 different countries.

Be Quick to Get Everyone on the Same Page

Making all this work required a unified process. Our team members were ready, enthusiastic, and, as YY noted, up to the task. As soon as he made the acquisition and restructuring announcements, emails flew in from members of our HR team, who were clearly excited about getting started and asking for details. Unlike the situation in the past, when we were first integrating IBM PC and Lenovo, we now had confidence that we could do this—we had the blueprint, and it was heartening to see the enthusiasm from people who could have legitimately been dreading the workload.

All of these external moves when we are in attack mode require constant internal readjustments. With every evolution of our business, YY and our leadership team have become known for aggressively restructuring our organization. While many companies take an "if it ain't broke, don't fix it" attitude, keeping their management structures in place despite the continually evolving global consumer landscape, we take a proactive approach, assessing whether or not we have the appropriate people placed in the right roles for growth and change. This is something that YY has insisted on ever since he first retook the wheel in 2009, so that we never rest on our laurels—we are always rethinking and pioneering ways to do it better.

This constant churning growth also means that our integration work is never done. Getting diversity exactly right—creating an inclusive yet functional environment for people from more than 50 nationalities—requires extraordinary patience and constant tweaking. Making history doesn't happen overnight. Thousands of people come and go, making it necessary to continually teach new people about the Lenovo Way. Even then, that recipe needs to be tweaked. As one of our Asian colleagues recently remarked, "We are never the experts. What you know in the past is past, and it may no longer be relevant. Always try to think of a different way."

That flexibility and willingness to adapt came into play recently as we came up with a new branding strategy. We wanted to balance simplicity with the idea that we have cool technology that people can do things with. We also wanted something that would resonate with the global youth market. The concept worked, but our tagline—For those who DO—became a problem when it was translated into Mandarin. While in English there is a common understanding that *do* means "to take action," the word has a slight negative connotation in the Chinese language, suggesting "the opposite of those who think."

"We jumped to that tagline too early, and we didn't work to get input from everyone around the world to ensure that the concept would work locally," said David Roman, our chief marketing officer, who was leading the project.

In the end, we just stuck with the English version. This was a good thing, because it helped our China team make the transition from thinking of Lenovo as a Chinese company to seeing us as what we really are—global. So we are using the English version of the logo and not translating it into Mandarin.

Follow the Blueprint for Sustainable, Long-Term Success

Challenges such as these come up regularly, but we use them as opportunities to learn. This is why we introduced *Fu Pan*.

As we mentioned earlier, *Fu Pan* is a Chinese term borrowed from the game of chess, or *weiqi*. It means replaying the chessboard or analyzing the strengths and opportunities for the next time a move is made so that it can be done better next time. We do this regularly, so that we have a better understanding of the moves we made and the actions we took to achieve something positive. It's a way to become creative and innovative in our problem solving.

Fu Pan, which is an example of our Fourth P, Practice, proved to be a particularly effective tool in India after we launched the Yoga, our laptop with a keyboard that could be rotated 360 degrees and converted into a tablet. The product was doing well in large retail stores, but sales were not consistent.

"While the individual store owner makes a difference, we don't normally see this kind of variance in sales. We were struggling to make sense of it," Amar Babu RK, our general manager for India, explained.[10]

A *Fu Pan* helped our India managers realize that the problem was not with the retail partners or the pricing of the product. Instead, the problem was that because of a lack of shelf space, the display stand that we'd included to show the Yoga's convertibility wasn't being used in many of the stores, so no one could see the product's chief design feature. We redesigned the stand to take up less room on the shelf, and as soon as we did so, we saw a rise in sales.

This is how we do things at Lenovo. We learn, we grow, and we evolve. We set a strategy and follow the principles, but we never stick rigidly to a process if it doesn't make sense for us. We are always prepared to change and diversify, whether that's through an internal reorganization, an acquisition, a product or marketing innovation, or a new business model. It's why we may not just stick to our Five Ps. We could add yet more Ps, or even Ts and Ds. *We learn from our past, but we change for our future.*

The global economy changes, consumer tastes evolve, and technology innovation moves along at warp speed, so we need to be nimble and willing to at least do all we can to learn and keep up with a business that will never stand still. But since the beginning, in that dusty guard shack on the outskirts of Beijing, we have had one distinct advantage over the rest: our people. They are the resource that we value above all, and the reason that we invest so much in training and developing at all levels of the organization. It's why we are so proud to be a part of this story and why we are so deeply committed to our ongoing journey at Lenovo.

The Chinese have a saying: "To cultivate trees, you need 10 years. To cultivate people, you need 100 years." That's fine with us, because we know how to be patient. Besides, Lenovo is going to be around for much, much longer.

From everything we have experienced and learned as a pioneering technology company over the past three decades, we know how to do this. In this highly competitive, ever-evolving environment, in which technology can become obsolete within a matter of months, we have figured out a way to innovate and thrive. We have done this before and learned, by trial, error, and persistence in moving forward as a truly global company, exactly how to assimilate many diverse cultures into one cohesive and effective team. Those difficult years following our acquisition of IBM PC gave us the blueprint, and as long as we live by the principles that we have developed—Plan, Perform, Prioritize, Practice, and Pioneer—not only can we repeat our success with the first major acquisition, but we will do it better, blending cultures and adapting new practices more quickly than ever before.

As in the past, industry observers have been quick to call our latest maneuvers risky. "I'm surprised Lenovo is getting into something this risky," one analyst told the *Wall Street Journal*, referring to the Motorola deal. "Lenovo is biting off more than it can chew."[11]

But anyone who has studied our history understands that the snake can indeed digest the elephant.

This is the Lenovo Way.

Lenovo Strategy Takeaways

- Be both local and global in your marketing strategy.

- Disciplined teams can move aggressively toward growth.

- When attacking new markets and product categories, take no prisoners.

- Pioneer new ideas, design innovations, and technology to thrive in an evolving global market.

- Not just any celebrity will do as your corporate spokesperson. Choose the right people to endorse and represent your brand.

- Being number one isn't enough. Continue to seek new pillars of growth.

- Replay the chessboard to learn from every success and failure.

Notes

Chapter 2

1. Ling Zhijun, *The Lenovo Affair: The Growth of China's Computer Giant and Its Takeover of IBM-PC* (Singapore: John Wiley & Sons [Asia] Ltd., 2005), p. 10.
2. Mure Dickie, "China's High-Tech Hero," *Chief Executive*, January 1, 2005.
3. Ling Zhijun, *Lenovo Affair*, p. 175.

Chapter 3

1. Ling Zhijun, *The Lenovo Affair: The Growth of China's Computer Giant and Its Takeover of IBM-PC* (Singapore: John Wiley & Sons [Asia] Ltd., 2005), p. 335.
2. "From Guard Shack to Global Giant: How Did Lenovo Become the World's Biggest Computer Company?" *The Economist*, January 13, 2013; http://www.economist.com/news/business/21569398-how-did-lenovo-become-worlds-biggest-computer-company-guard-shack-global-giant.
3. Steve Hamm, "Lenovo and IBM: East Meets West, Big-Time," *BusinessWeek*, May 8, 2005; http://www.businessweek.com/stories/2005-05-08/lenovo-and-ibm-east-meets-west-big-time.
4. Mure Dickie, "China's High-Tech Hero," *Chief Executive*, January 1, 2005.
5. Gunter K. Stahl and Kathrin Köster, "Lenovo-IBM: Bridging Cultures, Languages, and Time Zones," Case B, "Integration Challenges," WU Case Series, Wirtschafts Universität Wien, 2013; http://epub.wu.ac.at/3797/1/IBM_Lenovo_Case-B_WU-CaseSeries.pdf.
6. Ibid.
7. Ibid.
8. "From Guard Shack to Global Giant."
9. Stahl and Köster, "Lenovo-IBM."
10. Scott D. Seligman, *Chinese Business Etiquette: A Guide to Protocol, Manners, and Culture in the People's Republic of China* (New York: Warner, 1999); http://www.amazon.com/Chinese-Business-Etiquette-Protocol-thePeoples/dp/0446673870.

Chapter 4

1. Honggu Li, "The Path of Yang Yuanqing," *Life Week* 8 (2013).
2. Gunter K. Stahl and Kathrin Köster, "Lenovo-IBM: Bridging Cultures, Languages, and Time Zones," Case B, "Integration Challenges," WU

Case Series, Wirtschafts Universität Wien, 2013; http://epub.wu.ac.at
/3797/1/IBM_Lenovo_Case-B_WU-CaseSeries.pdf.
3. Ibid.

Chapter 5

1. Honggu Li, "The Path of Yang Yuanqing," *Life Week* 8 (2013).

Chapter 6

1. Honggu Li, "The Path of Yang Yuanqing," *Life Week* 8 (2013).

Chapter 9

1. China Information Technology Expo, 2014; http://eng.citexpo.org.
2. Craig Hill, "Lenovo to Launch Mobile Devices Facility in Central China," *China Daily Mail*, May 7, 2012; http://chinadailymail.com/2012/05/07/lenovo-to-launch-mobile-devices-facility-in-central-china/.
3. Leslie P. Norton, "Lenovo Attacks," *Barron's*, September 9, 2013; http://online.barrons.com/article/SB50001424052748704131804579053021180800410.html.
4. Eric Pfanner, "King of PCs, Lenovo Sets Smartphone Ambitions," *New York Times*, December 26, 2013; http://www.nytimes.com/2013/12/27/business/international/lenovo-no-1-in-pcs-aims-at-us-smartphone-market.html?_r=0.
5. Simon Montlake, "The Middle Way: Inside Lenovo's Bid to Build a Better Tablet," *Forbes*, November 18, 2013; http://www.forbes.com/sites/simonmontlake/2013/10/30/the-middle-way-inside-lenovos-bid-to-build-a-better-tablet/.
6. Paul Carsten and Soham Chatterjee, "Lenovo to Buy IBM's Low-End Server Unit for $2.3 Billion," Reuters, January 23, 2014; http://www.reuters.com/article/2014/01/23/us-ibm-server-lenovo-id USBREA0M01U20140123.
7. Nadia Damouni, Nicola Leske, and Gerry Shih, "Lenovo to Buy Google's Motorola in China's Largest Tech Deal," Reuters, January 29, 2014; http://www.reuters.com/article/2014/01/30/us-google-lenovo-id USBREA0S1YN20140130.
8. Pfanner, "King of PCs."
9. http://www.businessweek.com/stories/2010-08-06/do-multinationals-really-understand-globalization-businessweek-business-news-stock-market-and-financial-advice
10. Priyanka Sangani, "How Lenovo Plans to Checkmate Competition Using Chinese Chess Strategies," *India Economic Times*, March 14, 2014.
11. Juro Osawa and Lorraine Luk, "How Lenovo Built a Chinese Tech Giant," *Wall Street Journal*, January 30, 2014; http://online.wsj.com/news/articles/SB10001424052702303973704579352263128996836.

Acknowledgments

We sincerely thank our founder, Liu Chuanzhi, and our chairman and CEO, Yang Yuanqing, for building a truly great company and blazing a trail in our industry. We deeply appreciate their generous support, and we are forever grateful to all Lenovo employees, our colleagues, past and present, for their many contributions to the success of the Lenovo Way.

Gina Qiao

I would like to express my profound gratitude to my husband, Frank, my daughter, Georgia, and my mother and father. Through your selfless love, you have been beside me all these years, sharing my journey both in person and in spirit. I could not have done it without you. To my extended family members and dearest friends, I know how fortunate I am to have you in my life. Thank you for your unwavering support.

Yolanda Conyers

I would like to thank my loving husband, Chris. Honey, you are my rock. My darling boys, Cameron, Colton, and Christopher, I am overjoyed to have you in my life. Thank you, Mom, for your great example, and Dad, although you have passed, your lessons live on. To my beloved mother-in-law, I thank you for your strength. To my brothers, sisters, friends, and extended family, I so appreciate your love and support over the years. And thank you, God, for the countless blessings you have bestowed on me.

Gina and Yolanda

There is a special group of people who helped us make this book a reality.

In the early days, when we first had this idea, we deeply appreciated your coaching and mentoring to get this project off the ground.

It all started with Saj-nicole Joni, whose depth of experience as an author helped us facilitate our first writing session and fine-tune our vision for the book. She introduced us to Madeleine Morel, who then introduced us to our amazing writer.

We also thank Barry Rellaford, who inspired our confidence to write the book, and Greg Link, who shared with us the steps required to write a book from end to end.

Pam K. Henry was instrumental in helping us define the concept, as were Dick Jelinek, Laverne Council, and Margaret Keys, who provided great insights and guidance to further enhance our idea.

Robert Benowitz provided invaluable legal guidance and consulting for the book.

In the spirit of Lenovo, this book was a team effort. We'd like to thank the dedicated people who stayed up late at night and worked after hours to help us weave together the story that is told here. We call them our Lenovo Editing Team. This brilliant group includes John Stanley, Zhang Yan, Crystal Arrington, Yi Min, Nicole Li, and Norma Duff Greenwood. Stephanie Dubois, thank you for your concept for the beautiful book jacket and for jumping into the project and providing us with the beautiful photograph for the front cover.

And most especially, we thank our colleague and champion Jeffrey Shafer, who has supported this work since its inception. Your guidance and your eye for details have helped us bring to life *The Lenovo Way* in a way of which we can all be proud.

Tom Miller, thank you for your vision as an editor and for keeping us on track to produce a business book that is certain to help others replicate our successes and avoid the mistakes we made as we implemented the Lenovo Way. Your fine editing skills can be experienced on every single page of this book.

Our thanks also go to Carol Mann, who is the best agent on the planet.

Shuronda Robinson, our PR manager, has been with us every step of the way, demonstrating genuine care and concern for her clients.

Samantha Marshall, your superior writing skills have helped us to articulate what was in our hearts, minds, and memories about how *The Lenovo Way* came to be. Your cross-cultural expertise was a huge asset in bringing this story to life, and we thank you.

And finally, thanks to the entire production and publishing team at McGraw-Hill for making it happen in such a short time frame.

Index

About the Authors

Gina (Jian) Qiao, Senior Vice President of Human Resources at Lenovo, is the eighth-highest-ranking female executive in China, according to *Fortune China*. In many ways, Gina's steady climb from a secretary to the C-suite of the largest PC seller in the world reflects the extraordinary growth story of both Lenovo and China itself.

As leader of the technology giant's HR function, Gina oversees the organizational development, global talent, compensation, and benefits operations for more than 54,000 Lenovo employees across 60 countries, overseeing a corporate culture that is so diverse that six of the nine top leaders at the company are of different nationalities.

It was a long way to the top. Raised in the northeastern city of Dalian during China's Cultural Revolution, Gina remembers a time when the wealth, inclusiveness, and economic freedom that her country now enjoys were impossible to imagine. Her family members suffered greatly during this time. Her grandfather, a doctor who had been educated at Columbia University in New York in the 1930s and had practiced medicine in Boston before he was called back to help his country build hospitals, was arrested and imprisoned for more than two years as part of his "reeducation."

The repercussions affected everyone, including his children. In a family that reveres education, Gina's academically gifted father was barred from attending top-tier schools, although he eventually went on to become a mathematics professor at the University of Dalian.

Like most Chinese families before Deng Xiaoping's economic reforms took hold, the Qiaos had little. Food, especially meat, was scarce, and luxuries like new clothes were almost nonexistent. The small amount that Gina's parents had left from their meager resources was spent on books and school supplies. No one had to tell her the importance of studying hard, and Gina scored at the top of her class throughout her school years, earning a spot at the prestigious Fudan University in Shanghai.

Gina obtained a bachelor's degree in management science, and, after graduating in 1990, she gained an entry-level position within Lenovo's planning department. Because of her knowledge of Lenovo's computer technology and her ability to communicate well in Mandarin, she was given the job of writing progress reports to the government and explaining why the business needed access to U.S. currency—at the time, the renminbi, the Chinese currency, was nonconvertible.

After six months in this role, Gina joined the secretarial pool for the chairman's office. While she is the first to admit that she was not cut out to be a secretary, it was there that Gina learned the art of prioritizing and multitasking, impressing the leadership with her diligence and building lasting relationships with the founding partners that would become crucially important later in her career.

Lenovo gave her not only a career but also a home. As a young university graduate, neither Gina nor her family had the funds to pay for accommodations in Beijing, so she lived in Lenovo's employee dorms, sharing a small space with four other colleagues. Two years later, a company-endorsed mortgage enabled her to buy her first apartment, in a housing complex built by Lenovo and also inhabited by 71 of her colleagues.

Before long, she moved on to Lenovo's marketing and branding divisions, helping to drive the company's growth in market share and its rise to leadership in China's PC market. She distinguished herself as an award-winning marketing manager and devised many advertising campaigns, some of which Lenovo still uses to this day.

By 2000, as Lenovo became the dominant player in China with a market share of 27 percent, CEO Yang Yuanqing (known as YY) decided that it was time to develop new goals for the company: to transform it into a diversified and global business. In 2002, YY asked Gina to help run the increasingly vital function of human resources. While she was reluctant to leave marketing, which she loved, Gina embraced the challenge and began the arduous process of recruiting more multinational talent to Lenovo to help support its global ambitions.

In 2004, Gina was involved in the yearlong negotiations to acquire IBM's PC division, a deal that finally closed on May 1, 2005. In October 2005, with the newly merged businesses doing better than expected, she moved to New York for a short-term assignment to design the organization, titles, compensation, benefits, and culture integration for the newly merged operation. She then followed the executive team to Singapore in June 2006, where she ran human resources for Lenovo's Asia-Pacific region.

Her task was daunting; the language and cultural barriers were profound. Few Lenovo executives had international experience, much less English language skills, including Gina. But Gina's collegial attitude and her commitment to learning English and immersing herself in unfamiliar corporate styles and cultures eventually won over the IBM PC employees.

In September 2007, Gina, along with her husband and her teenage daughter, relocated to Lenovo's U.S. headquarters in Raleigh, North Carolina, to serve as the Global Consumer Business HR head, living and working alongside her Lenovo International colleagues, learning their best practices, and incorporating those practices into the Lenovo Way. In 2009, while still in Raleigh, she led Lenovo's strategy and planning department, where she was responsible for helping to define, articulate, and implement the company's overarching global strategy, working closely with Lenovo's board of directors and executive committee. In 2011, she was promoted to senior vice president in charge of global HR.

Gina has since returned to Beijing with her husband, Frank Zhang, leaving her daughter, Georgia, to study art and economics at the University of North Carolina at Chapel Hill. Gina also began a blog on Weibo, the Chinese online social media platform, writing about her daily life as a busy female executive and mother; her blog has more than three million subscribers across China. She is regularly sought out as a speaker at colleges and corporate campuses throughout the world.

Gina holds an executive MBA from the China-Europe International Business School; she is also a 2012 graduate of the University of Michigan's Advanced Human Resource Executive Training.

In 2012 and 2013, she was recognized as one of the top 10 business-women in *Fortune China* and *China Entrepreneur* magazine.

Today, Gina speaks fluent English, leading meetings and giving speeches to thousands of employees, and motivating her American team with jokes and stories about her own struggles to adapt to the dramatic changes that have occurred throughout her career at Lenovo.

Yolanda Conyers is Vice President of Global HR Operations as well as the Chief Diversity Officer for Lenovo. As the first global diversity officer for a Chinese-heritage company, Yolanda is a pioneer in the field of human resources and one of the chief architects of the cultural integration of computer giants Lenovo and the IBM PC division. Nothing in the textbooks could have prepared her for the challenges of integrating two such widely divergent corporate styles from opposite sides of the globe—Lenovo, the successful Chinese company formerly known as Legend, and American icon IBM's PC division. Early in the merger, Lenovo committed to finding innovative and realistic approaches to cultural integration and diversity; these have been critical in enabling its top global talent to partner seamlessly within this new phase of growth, and Yolanda, sponsored by Lenovo's leadership executive committee, has played a significant role in helping to implement these changes. Yolanda led the launch of the Lenovo Way, a worldwide corporate culture initiative that has become a blueprint for business diversity across industries.

Born the youngest of seven children in the small town of Port Arthur, Texas, Yolanda was raised in a predominantly African American neighborhood by a working mother, while her father worked on numerous merchant ships that traveled internationally, remaining at sea for months at a time. Although he had no formal education, her father gained the knowledge and skills he needed to become the ship's chief steward, eventually earning a middle-class salary to support his family. His dedication to learning, his wisdom, and the stories he brought back from far-flung corners of the globe inspired Yolanda and awakened in her a desire to keep expanding her knowledge, as well as a curiosity about other cultures that remains with her to this day.

Yolanda became the first and only member of her family to receive both a bachelor's and a master's degree. During her freshman year studying computer science at Lamar University's college of engineering in Texas, from which she graduated a member of the Cap and Gown Senior Honor Society, she caught the attention of Texas Instruments, which hired her for three semesters of internships. Upon graduation, TI gave the young software engineer a full-time position.

In 1991, Yolanda moved to computer giant Dell, where she was the first African American female engineer hired by the company and where she had various roles in Product Development, Sales, Customer Service, Human Resources, and Procurement/Global Supply Chain. During her tenure at Dell, she earned an executive MBA in international business and won numerous professional accolades, including the YWCA Woman of the Year in Science and Technology, the Texas Legislative Black Caucus Outstanding Texan in Business, and the Women of Color in Technology National Award for Special Achievement.

But health problems before, during, and after the birth of her second son in 2005 followed by time away on maternity leave gave Yolanda some distance from and perspective on the company that she'd served for 15 years, helping her to realize the paramount importance of a work/life balance. This enabled her to see that it was time for a change, and she resigned from Dell and spent a year focusing on herself and her family in order to determine where her true passion lay.

In 2007, Yolanda was recruited by Lenovo and asked to take on one of the most significant challenges facing the company: global culture and diversity integration. That year, in order to better understand the culture and practices of her new colleagues in Asia, she relocated to Beijing for a short-term assignment, leading the design and implementation of strategies to integrate the complex fabric of Eastern and Western cultures. A year later, she was asked to expand her responsibilities by leading and creating programs to develop top global talent, foster a high-performance culture, and build employee capacity and alignment to drive better business outcomes.

Traveling extensively among Lenovo offices throughout China, the United States, and Europe, Yolanda has continued to be the chief diversity officer. Her responsibilities have included redefining what diversity means at Lenovo and within the industry at large, and integrating Lenovo employees from all cultures and backgrounds to promote teamwork across cultures. She has worked closely with the Leadership Executive Committee, including the chairman and CEO, her HR peers, and the global team, to improve understanding, respect, and communication among the wide range of nationalities and backgrounds that exist in the organization as a result of the IBM PC acquisition. This work ultimately led to the creation of the Lenovo Way, which has been embedded in the culture of the organization from the top down.

In 2009, Yolanda made the decision to move her family to Beijing for a longer-term assignment. Being based in China allowed her to work more closely with Lenovo's most senior leadership, including Chairman Liu. Moreover, during this critical period in Lenovo's global integration, the move also lessened her overseas travel schedule and enabled her to spend more time with her husband and her two young boys. She dedicated herself to the study of Mandarin and made a point of visiting different parts of China and other countries in Asia with her family in order to experience as much of her newly adopted home as she could.

In 2012, Yolanda was asked to take on another complex project: the overall reorganization of global HR operations. While continuing to oversee diversity, she has been given the task of completing the alignment of all Lenovo's employees into a single HR system, globalizing processes in order to ensure consistent day-to-day management and increased accuracy, speed, and efficiency in support of the business. In 2012, Yolanda also graduated from the University of Michigan's Advanced Human Resource Executive Program.

By far Yolanda's proudest accomplishment is the success and happiness of her family and the journey of personal growth that she and they shared during their almost 3½-year stay in Beijing. In 2009, Yolanda was declared Working Mother of the Year by *Working Mother* magazine, and she was featured on the *Today* show as a result. This is an achievement that she attributes to the unwavering support of her husband, Chris, and the love of her three sons, Christopher, Cameron, and Colton.